YOU CAN BEGIN AGAIN

YOU CAN BEGIN AGAIN

No Matter What,
It's Never Too Late

JOYCE MEYER

Faith Words

NEW YORK • BOSTON • NASHVILLE

Unless otherwise noted Scriptures are taken from *The Amplified Bible* (AMP). *The Amplified Bible, Old Testament*, copyright © 1965, 1987 by The Zondervan Corporation. *The Amplified New Testament*, copyright © 1954, 1958, 1987 by The Lockman Foundation. Used by permission.

Scriptures noted (THE MESSAGE) are taken from *The Message: The Prophets* by Eugene Peterson. Copyright © 2000 by Eugene H. Peterson. NavPress Publishing Group, P.O. Box 35001, Colorado Springs, CO 80935. Used by permission.

Scriptures noted (NIV) are taken from the *Holy Bible: New International Version*®. Copyright © 1973, 1978, 1984 by International Bible Society. Used by permission of Zondervan Publishing House. All rights reserved.

Scripture quotations marked (NLT) are taken from the *Holy Bible*, New Living Translation, Copyright © 1996. Used by permission of Tyndale House Publishers, Inc., Wheaton, Illinois 60189. All rights reserved.

FaithWords
Hachette Book Group
237 Park Avenue
New York, NY 10017

www.faithwords.com

Printed in the United States of America

RRD-H

First Edition: April 2014

10 9 8 7 6 5 4 3 2 1

FaithWords is a division of Hachette Book Group, Inc.
The FaithWords name and logo are trademarks of Hachette Book Group, Inc.

The Hachette Speakers Bureau provides a wide range of authors for speaking events. To find out more, go to www.hachettespeakersbureau.com or call (866) 376-6591.

The publisher is not responsible for websites (or their content) that are not owned by the publisher.

Library of Congress Cataloging-in-Publication Data

Meyer, Joyce, 1943–

You can begin again : No matter what, it's never too late / Joyce Meyer.

pages cm

ISBN 978-1-4555-1741-1 (hardcover) — ISBN 978-1-4555-8201-3 (large print hardcover) — ISBN 978-1-61113-261-8 (audio CD) — ISBN 978-1-4789-5251-0 (audio download) — ISBN 978-1-4555-1742-8 (ebook) 1. Change (Psychology—Religious aspects—Christianity. 2. Determination (Personality trait) I. Title.

BV4599.5.C44M49 2014

248.8'6—dc23

2013030529

Therefore if any person is [ingrafted] in Christ (the Messiah) he is a new creation (a new creature altogether); the old [previous moral and spiritual condition] has passed away. Behold, the fresh and new has come!

2 Corinthians 5:17

CONTENTS

Introduction   ix

PART I
New Beginnings

CHAPTER 1   Help! I'm Stuck!   3

CHAPTER 2   Why Today Is Different   13

CHAPTER 3   Getting Past Your Past   23

CHAPTER 4   It's Never Too Late   34

CHAPTER 5   All You Need Is A Moment   45

PART II
What's Stopping You?

CHAPTER 6   Did You Pay For That?   57

CHAPTER 7   Who Do You Think You Are?!?   66

CHAPTER 8   Finding The YOU In Bea-YOU-tiful   80

CHAPTER 9   Defeating Unexpected Giants   95

CHAPTER 10 On Your Mark...Get Set...GO!   108

PART III
Today Is Your Day

CHAPTER 11 Little Things Make A Big Difference   123

CHAPTER 12 Quitting Isn't An Option   135

CHAPTER 13 Don't Waste Your Mistakes   144

CHAPTER 14 When All Things Become New   154

CHAPTER 15 Plan B: B Stands For Better   166

CHAPTER 16 A New Dream   178

CHAPTER 17 The Greatest Story Ever Told   187

Afterword   197

Prayer of Salvation   199

INTRODUCTION

History (with a touch of folklore) tells the story of Great Britain's larger-than-life prime minister, Winston Churchill, boldly delivering a one-sentence speech to his countrymen. Legend has it that Churchill stood before a hushed crowd during the darkest days of World War II and boldly declared: "Never, never, never, never give up." He then turned and sat down, confident those six words were enough.

Though historians record that Churchill actually offered a few more paragraphs that day, it was this one bold sentence that stuck in the minds of the struggling, battle-weary citizens. *Never, never, never, never give up!*

As a minister of the Gospel for nearly 38 years, I'm used to standing in front of crowds, but I have to admit, I've never given a one-sentence sermon. I have a feeling those who come to hear me might not be as impressed as the British crowd that day—they might expect a little more.

But if I were bold enough to give a one-sentence message right now—if I had only a few seconds to share with you one idea that might change your life—here's what I would say:

> *Whoever you are, wherever you are, whatever you've been through, it's never too late to begin again.*

I believe this one sentence is more than a speech or a sermon; it is one of the core messages of the Bible. Regardless of your past failure or your present struggle, God offers you a new beginning. Fresh starts aren't the exception; they're the rule. We see them all throughout the Word of God. For example:

- Far from his potential, wandering on the back side of the desert, Moses is called to lead a nation. *Fresh start!*
- A victim of her reputation, known only as the harlot, Rahab is rescued and given a noble name in the lineage of Christ. *Fresh start!*
- Stuck in a dead-end job tending sheep, David is anointed the next king of Israel. *Fresh start!*
- Widowed, alone, and with nowhere to go, Ruth is given a brand-new, better-than-imagined life. *Fresh start!*
- Ashamed, having given in to fear and denied the Lord, Peter is forgiven and inspired to preach at Pentecost. *Fresh start!*
- Caught in a trap of dead religion, persecuting the early Christians, Paul is transformed and called to write much of the New Testament. *Fresh start!*

Do you see the pattern? Time after time, story after story, page after page—God offers a new beginning, and His people make the most of it. The circumstances change, and the stories vary, but the grace of God never wavers. God always offers a new chance. A new opportunity. A new life.

However, as I travel from city to city, preaching the Word, I meet many individuals who are still living in darkness. For some, it's a darkness of pain—hurt has them frozen in their tracks, groping for answers. For others, it's a darkness of disappointment—life hasn't turned out how they planned, and they feel lost and unsure. Still for others, darkness comes as a cloud of loneliness, fear, boredom, uncertainty, worry, or despair.

It is my heart's desire to see people set free and living the new, overcoming, joy-filled life that Jesus came to give them. I know firsthand how freeing this can be. You see, not only have I met people stuck in uncertainty, I've been stuck there a time or two myself. I know what it's like to be so worried you'll either do the wrong thing or, just as bad, do nothing at all.

I imagine you've experienced this feeling before too. It seems that we all have, at one time or another, stared at a roadblock in life and wondered, *Is this it? Am I finished? Should I give up? What do I do now?* But Scripture tells us the Word of God is a "lamp to my feet and a light to my path" (Psalm 119:105). This means that no matter how dark your surroundings, you never lose your way. God will guide you to your destiny—it's never too late.

Here is the key: You have to take a step. New beginnings don't happen on an escalator, they happen along a path. In faith, you make progress by taking one step at a time. If you are determined to succeed in life, God's grace will enable you to do what may seem impossible to your natural thinking. God has promised to do His part, but you have an important part to play as well.

If you know what it's like to be far from your potential; to suffer from a less-than-stellar reputation; to find yourself stuck in a dead-end job; to feel abandoned or alone; to live with regret or shame; or just to wonder what your next step might be, let this book be a new beginning for you.

I've divided the content into three sections: *New Beginnings, What's Stopping You?* and *Today Is Your Day.* These topics come directly from 2 Corinthians 5:17, the banner verse for fresh starts. In each section, you'll discover amazing people who seized their chance to begin again. Their courage, boldness, and determination will lift your spirit and build your faith. In addition to encouraging stories, you'll find practical steps from the Word that will help you live out your fresh start. These truths will provide a strong foundation for your future.

But more than anything else, I pray that every word in this book will help you discover God Himself. Deep and abiding relationship with Him is the foundation and source of every new beginning. He is the ultimate prize, and we must never forget that true joy and happiness are found only in Him.

As you read these pages, I pray you see that God loves you with an everlasting love (Jeremiah 31:3), He is with you now and always (Deuteronomy 31:6), and He desires to give you an abundant, over-coming, joy-filled life (John 10:10).

That life can be yours today if you'll receive it. Just remember...

Whoever you are, wherever you are, whatever you've been through, it's never too late to begin again.

YOU
CAN
BEGIN
AGAIN

PART I

New Beginnings

Therefore if any person is [ingrafted] in Christ (the Messiah) he is a new creation (a new creature altogether)...

2 Corinthians 5:17; Part I

CHAPTER 1

Help! I'm Stuck!

"Chords that were broken will vibrate once more."
—Fanny Crosby

A young minister who we will call Eric decided to take piano lessons. Due to his profession, learning to play music just made sense. If his worship leader called in sick, or if a musician backed out moments before a service, he would be able to step in and play. Eric, the piano-playing preacher; he smiled at the thought of it.

Determined, Eric took lessons faithfully for over five years. Every week, he showed up for his Tuesday lesson with a local piano instructor, and every morning he rose early to log diligent practice time. By his own admission, he was far from a natural. The learning was slow-going and the progress was incremental, but with the patience of his teacher and his own desire for improvement, Eric made steady strides toward his goal.

One day, his piano instructor, a local legend with a kind disposition and a no-nonsense work ethic, announced that she scheduled Eric to play in a countywide competition. He would be required to play a full concerto in front of a panel of judges who would grade his performance. Though Eric was hesitant to play in such a venue, his instructor insisted, explaining that the pressure would be good for him.

The Saturday morning of the competition arrived. Eric was extremely nervous as he showed up to his assigned destination, ready to get the whole thing over with. There was an empty practice room available, so Eric practiced his piece repeatedly until it was finally time to face the judges.

As he entered the room, Eric greeted the three accomplished judges anxiously and made his way to the baby grand piano. Though he was perfectly comfortable preaching in front of large crowds, the thought of playing in front of these three musical experts unnerved him. After exhaling slowly, he placed his fingers above the keys and began to play. To his delight, the first few measures of music came out perfectly. It appeared the months of practice had paid off as his fingers touched each key flawlessly, moving from sheer muscle memory. His teacher smiled in the back of the room, and Eric visibly relaxed as he worked his way through the introduction of the assigned piece.

But his confidence didn't last long—moments later, musical disaster struck. His hands froze over the keys, not knowing where to go next. Inexplicably, Eric, the piano-playing preacher, had forgotten the next note.

After a pause that seemed like an eternity, he guessed at a new note, but it was not even close to being correct. Eric winced at the ugly sound that came from the piano. Out of the corner of his eye, he saw the frowning judges marking his mistake. Embarrassed, he shook his head and plowed into another chord, but it was even worse. Eric was hopelessly lost now. Nervous. Confused. Searching.

Not knowing what to do, Eric stopped playing all together. Dejected, he hung his head low. *"How could this have happened?"* he thought. *"I practiced so hard!"* Looking at the panel of judges, he said sheepishly, "I'm really sorry. I seem to have forgotten the piece. I'm afraid that if I keep going, it's only going to get worse. Should I just stop here?"

Should I Just Stop Here?

Do you know what that feels like? Have you ever found yourself so stuck that you didn't know how to proceed? Stuck in a stagnant marriage. Stuck in a dead-end job. Stuck in an unhealthy lifestyle. Stuck in an uncertainty about your future. You practiced, you prepared, you even prayed, but it feels like you're going nowhere. Maybe you know exactly what it's like to think, *"I'm afraid that if I keep going, it's only going to get worse. Should I just stop here?"*

I know what it feels like too. There have been times in my life when I felt like I had hit a dead end. Times I thought if I kept going in the direction I was going, I was just going to make matters worse. I've run into roadblocks just like you have. There are just some days and some situations that cause us all to freeze in our tracks. I think that's why I take such comfort in the way Eric's story ends.

You see, in the tension of the moment, Eric's piano instructor walked toward him from her place in the back of the room. The judges shifted in their chairs as the teacher calmly approached her discouraged student. When she reached him, she bent over and whispered three sentences into his ear that changed his entire disposition: "Don't worry," she said. "It's not too late. You can begin again."

Patting his shoulder reassuringly, the teacher winked kindly and then returned to her seat in the back of the room. For my friend, everything changed at that moment. Though he was stuck, he discovered he didn't have to stay stuck. In the midst of despair, those words were exactly what he needed to hear. *Don't worry. It's not too late. You can begin again.*

It never occurred to Eric that he would be able to start the piece over. Up to this point, the events of his entire life taught him that mistakes equaled failure, and there was no coming back from failure. This was why he worked so hard, and this was why he was so devastated by his predicament. But this opportunity to try again changed the temperature in the room that day. Eric calmed himself, started over, and played freer than he had ever played before. There was no longer any pressure to convince the judges he was perfect. They saw him lose his way but allowed him the chance to find it again. And that is exactly what he did. He played the piece beautifully the second time through, finishing to the applause of the understanding judges and his delighted teacher.

The Whisper Of Grace

When I heard that story, I couldn't help thinking that Eric's piano teacher whispered something eternal to him that day. She whispered the language of heaven. She whispered grace. In a moment of desperation, to an anxious soul that was helplessly stuck, she whispered what God whispers to us all: "Don't worry. It's not too late. You can begin again."

I think that at one time or another, all of us get lost in the middle of our song. A failed marriage, a broken dream, a disappointing career, a financial setback, or a family struggle causes us to hang our heads low and wonder where things went wrong. We assume others are watching us like a panel of unforgiving judges, marking our missed notes with enthusiasm. Even worse, we assume God is the head judge, giving disapproving attention to our forgotten melody. With each mistake or setback, we grow ever more nervous, certain we'll receive a failing grade.

But the Bible gives us quite a different picture of God. Regardless of what you've been told, God doesn't give up on you when you get stuck. He's not surprised by your situation, and He isn't mad at you. God doesn't give a failing grade and then callously move on to the next

> *Regardless of what you've been told, God doesn't give up on you when you get stuck.*

student. These thoughts about God are lies from the enemy. The devil would have you believe that God is distant, disappointed, or ready to punish you when you make mistakes. Because Satan wants to destroy your life (John 10:10), he repeats these lies as many times as it takes for you to believe them.

Lies That Keep You Stuck

The wrong view of God will keep you stuck. Whether you're stuck in pain, dysfunction, loneliness, uncertainty, overwhelming debt, or fear, the devil will lie to you about God in order to keep you stuck in that place forever. The first lie we believe is that God is mad at us. We picture God sitting up in heaven frowning at our failure, like an intimidating Driver's Ed teacher who sighs loudly when you fail to parallel-park correctly.

The devil knows that if you fall for his lie that God is angry, and very disappointed with you, he can keep you from having a real relationship with God. You'll spend your days trying to earn God's approval or impress Him with your best actions. You'll get stuck in a religious, fear-based cycle and never experience the deep, abiding relationship God wants to have with you. And you certainly won't turn to the Lord when you find yourself unsure of where to go or what to do next. But look at what Hebrews 4:16 says about how you can approach God:

> Let us then fearlessly and confidently and boldly draw near to the throne of grace (the throne of God's unmerited favor to us sinners), that we may receive mercy [for our failures] and find grace to help in good time for every need [appropriate help and well-timed help, coming just when we need it].

Not only can you come to God when you're stuck, you can come to Him "fearlessly" and "confidently." You won't find a harsh, cruel, angry God; you'll find His "mercy" and "grace." He loves you, and He's waiting to help you in your time of need!

Another lie the devil will tell you is that you're on your own. He wants you to rely on yourself rather than on God, so he tries to get you to think that God has abandoned you. This is a lie that many buy into much too easily. It appeals to our independent nature, and we end up thinking things like, "I made my bed, now I've got to lie in it," or "Well, I made this mess, so I guess I've got to clean it up." And then we go about the pathetic process of self-improvement.

Now, I do believe that we should take steps to improve our lives, but these things never take the place of complete dependence on God. When we try to solve our problems independently from God, we're like children trying to clean up the spill before Mommy or Daddy sees it—we usually just make things worse.

Proverbs 3:5–6 says: "Lean on, trust in, and be confident in the Lord with all your heart and mind and do not rely on your own insight or understanding. In all your ways know, recognize, and acknowledge Him, and He will direct and make straight and plain your paths." Notice it doesn't say, "In a *few* of your ways acknowledge Him," and it doesn't say, "In *most* of your ways acknowledge Him." The Word of God says, "In *all* your ways, know, recognize, and acknowledge Him."

That means nothing is off-limits. Good or bad, clean or dirty, lost or found, every part of your life can be given to God. You can trust Him with your life even when you're stuck in a situation and you're not sure how you got into it, and certainly don't know how to get out of it! Don't listen to the lies of the enemy. You don't have to hide from God out of fear that He is angry or disappointed, and you don't have to find a way to move forward in your own strength. You can trust God to show you the way.

> *Good or bad, clean or dirty, lost or found, every part of your life can be given to God.*

The Redeemer

Ruth knew what it was like to be stuck. The Bible tells us it seemed as if her entire life crashed down around her. Her husband of 10 years died unexpectedly, Naomi (her mother-in-law) was moving away to another country, and Ruth had nowhere to go. As you may well know, sometimes it's the unforeseen events that do the most damage, cruelly shattering the dreams we once had. This is what happened to Ruth; she was waking up to a harsh new reality.

It would have been easy for Ruth to give up and stay stuck. She could have set up camp right where she was and lived in that trauma forever. No one would have blamed her. She faced a pain she didn't ask for, a pain that was deep and tragic. She was a victim of her circumstances—circumstances that threatened to ruin her life. The choice Ruth had to make was whether or not to stay a victim.

But Ruth chose to break free. She told Naomi in Ruth 1:16, "...Urge me not to leave you or to turn back from following you; for where you go I will go, and where you lodge I will lodge. Your people shall be my people and your God my God." Ruth boldly set out on a journey with Naomi and God. She chose a new family, a new place, and a new future. Ruth realized it wasn't too late to start over.

Though the story of Ruth began in sadness, it ends in great joy. In her new life, Ruth meets a man named Boaz. Boaz is a kind man with great wealth, and he falls in love with Ruth. He provides for her and he protects her. The book of Ruth tells us that Boaz became a redeemer for Ruth. He paid a great price to build a new life for her—a life greater than anything she had imagined.

As you read these pages, I believe God wants to speak to you through the life of Ruth. Your struggle is real, and I know it hasn't been easy. No one would blame you if you stayed right where you are, letting life go by without you. Maybe an unexpected loss has stopped you in your tracks. Maybe a sudden life-change has you longing for the past. Maybe a broken relationship or an unexpected

> *You can stay stuck, dwelling on negative thoughts and living in worry and fear, or you can believe God has something greater for you.*

betrayal has you questioning everything you once believed to be true.

But you, like Ruth, have a choice to make today. You can stay stuck, dwelling on negative thoughts and living in worry and fear, or you can believe God has something greater for you. It's no accident you picked up this book; I believe that God is whispering to you right now. He wants you to know that your life isn't over. He has a plan and a purpose for you, and He wants you to discover a life greater than anything you could have imagined. I recently heard someone say, "If you're not dead, then you're not done!" Why not claim today as a day of new beginnings!

Ruth's life is more than a good story; it's God's message to anyone who needs to begin again. Boaz is a foreshadow of Jesus. Just as Ruth became Boaz's wife, the Word says we are the Bride of Christ (Revelation 22:17). Just as Boaz gave Ruth a new life, the Word says that we have a new life in Christ (2 Corinthians 5:17). Just as Ruth was redeemed, the Word says that we are also redeemed (Galatians 3:13).

No matter what wrong you have done, or what wrong thing has happened to you, God sees you right where you are, and He is your Redeemer. He's making a new way for you. If you'll reject the lies of the enemy, ignore the judgment of others, and put away your own fears and worries, you'll hear the voice of God today. It's not a shout, and it's not a lecture. It's a whisper. A whisper that is kind and reassuring. A whisper that says, *Don't worry. It's not too late. You can begin again.*

Summary:

- The Grace of God says, "It's never too late to begin again."
- Lies from the enemy will keep you stuck in your past.

- God isn't angry with you, and He isn't distant from you.
- You can approach God fearlessly and confidently—He offers mercy and grace in your time of need.
- You have the choice to stay stuck or believe God for a new beginning.

A Time I Almost Got Stuck

Early in our ministry, I remember we had our program on a particular television station once a week. At the time, I felt this was a key station for us to be on. One day, the executives of the station called us and said they were canceling our contract. The only reason they gave us was they were making some new programming choices and they decided to drop our broadcast. I was really upset about the news. I wondered how it was possible that they could just tear up our contract. This was an injustice, and though I was very disappointed, there was nothing we could do about it.

In the days that followed, as I was praying about the situation, I felt God speak to my heart and tell me to forgive the people who made this decision. Now, I have to be honest: I didn't really want to forgive them. I was upset and disappointed, but by God's grace, I chose to obey the Lord and forgive those who treated us poorly. Rather than get stuck in anger and disappointment, I trusted God and just let it go.

About a year later, this same station contacted us and asked us to come back on their station. Not once a week, not twice a week... they wanted to broadcast our program every single day! At the time, this was a huge opportunity for the ministry, and it still stands as a testimony of what God can do when we turn situations over to Him.

Had I not obeyed what the Lord was speaking to me about forgiveness, I would have been stuck in anger and bitterness. I firmly believe that we would not have been given that new opportunity if I hadn't trusted the Lord and moved past my hurt.

Today, our broadcast can be seen by two-thirds of the world. God has brought us a long way from those early ministry years, but one thing hasn't changed: We still depend on Him, and we still seek to obey Him every day and in everything He speaks to us.

Seeking God's will, listening for God's voice, obeying what God says—these things will help you get unstuck every time!

CHAPTER 2

Why Today Is Different

"Take the first step in faith. You don't have to see the whole staircase, just take the first step."

—Martin Luther King, Jr.

No one spoke a word. The tension in the air was so thick you could cut it with a knife. The crowd gathered in stunned silence, wondering: Is she going to die? Are they really going to kill her? Can Jesus save her? In the center of the temple court was the ugly source of the drama. Scribes and Pharisees, standing over a woman caught in adultery, stones in hand, asking defiantly: "The Law commanded us that such [women— offenders] shall be stoned to death. But what do You say [to do with her—what is Your sentence]?"

No one stirred as the fate of this battered, sobbing woman hung in the balance. The accusers were ready; the accused stood guilty; the punishment seemed inevitable. That's when Jesus said it—words so profound they caused the law-enforcers to pause, to look inward instead of outward. While stooping down and writing in the dirt, Jesus proclaimed, "Let him who is without sin among you be the first to throw a stone at her."

Tension. Wonder. Silence.

The disciples stood on alert. Bystanders prayed silently. Mothers covered the eyes of their children. Then it happened. Slowly, one by one, the angry religious officials dropped their stones and sulked away. With her pardon secured, the crowd let out a slow, collective sigh of relief. There would be no public stoning today. Not if Jesus had anything to do with it.

When I read John 8:1–11, that is what I envision. This story is not just a casual anecdote; it's a heroic, dramatic, lifesaving encounter with the living God. This is why the crowds loved Jesus: He never ceased to amaze them! But it was more than just the power and wisdom of Jesus that drew people to Him; it was the fact that He offered something new.

In the Old Testament, the people lived according to the Law. Their only connection to God was through priests and by a series of rules and rituals that kept them at arm's length from their Heavenly Father. But Jesus came as Immanuel (God with us). He offered a new way to relate to God: direct, intimate, personal. And with a new way to relate to God came a new way to live for Him: all mistakes, all sins, and wrongdoing could be forgiven, and each day offered a new beginning.

What Jesus says to the sinful woman after the scribes and Pharisees dropped the stones and walked away is a perfect example of the new life we find in Christ. John 8:10–11 says:

> *When Jesus raised Himself up, He said to her, Woman, where are your accusers? Has no man condemned you?*
>
> *She answered, No one, Lord!*
>
> *And Jesus said, I do not condemn you either. Go on your way and from now on sin no more.*

Moments earlier, this woman's life was in jeopardy due to her sins; there was no doubt she was guilty. The Law demanded payment, and she expected punishment. But Jesus offered something greater: a promise.

He looked at her and said the same thing that He says to each of us today: "Go on your way and from now on sin no more." Jesus wasn't excusing the wrongdoing, and He wasn't ignoring the destructive power that sin can have in our lives. Instead, He was offering a new life that was free of sin. He was saying to this broken woman: *Today can be different!*

This is the same thing that God says to you. *Today can be different!* Today can be a place to begin again! If your life has become a life full of worry, fear, negative thinking, sickness, despair, sin, and regret, today can be different. You don't have to give in to those things that would keep you from the life God has for you—you may have in your past, but you don't have to in your future. You can begin again! Jesus is sending away your accusers and offering you a new chance today. Today can be a brand-new start.

> *Jesus is sending away your accusers and offering you a new chance today. Today can be a brand-new start.*

Four Ways To Make Today Different From Yesterday

1. *Make Up Your Mind To Live Differently*

If you've been to my conferences or read my books before (especially *Power Thoughts*), you know that one of my favorite sayings is, "Where the mind goes, the man follows." The way you think determines the way you live. If you think you are going to be defeated, then you're going to have a defeated attitude. If you think you're going to make the same mistakes you've made in the past, then you're pointing your life in the wrong direction. Too many people go through life as prisoners of their own thoughts. They become subject to any and every thought that enters their minds.

In order to experience God's plan for your life, begin by receiving God's grace (His power and ability) and taking every thought that stands against the Word of God captive. Defeated, negative thoughts are what I call "stinking thinking" and have no place in the thought life of a child of God. Yesterday, you may have let your mind focus on the negative—what you can't do, how badly you've messed up, all the things that could go wrong—but today you can submit your mind to the Word of God. Today, you can decide what thoughts you are going to think.

Imagine a bank robber has robbed a bank and is fleeing the scene of the crime. The police officers on duty don't just let him run around the city causing chaos and wreaking havoc on the general population. They hunt him down and take him captive.

With this picture in your mind, look at what Paul says in 2 Corinthians 10:5: "...We take captive every thought to make it obedient to Christ" (NIV). Just as you want the police department to guard your city, God wants you to guard your mind. It's only after you have pursued and taken every negative thought captive that you can live the life God has called you to live. Our minds must be renewed if we desire to enjoy the good life that God has provided for us in Christ (Romans 12:2).

With the help of the Holy Spirit, you can change your thoughts today. You can choose to live differently.

> But we have the mind of Christ (the Messiah) and do hold the thoughts (feelings and purposes) of His heart. (1 Corinthians 2:16)

2. Praise Your Way To Victory

In Acts 16, Paul and Silas were flogged and thrown in prison for preaching the Word of God. Unlike the woman caught in adultery, who needed rescue because of her sin, these two missionaries needed rescue because of their zeal for God. You see, obstacles in your life don't always come because you did something wrong. Sometimes God will allow you to go through certain difficulties so that His glory can be revealed. If you will be faithful in the uncertainty, He'll do something greater in your life than you could have imagined.

This is what happened with Paul and Silas. Their surroundings were dreary. Their circumstances were disappointing. Their prospects were discouraging. The only thing in their situation not depressing was their attitude. Paul and Silas didn't blame God for their imprisonment; they worshipped Him in spite of it. Even though their bodies were locked up, their spirits soared free as they sang praise and worship songs to God.

And they didn't just praise for a few minutes; they praised for as long as it took. Verse 25 says they were praying and singing hymns at "about midnight" when God shook the jail cell and they were freed. They didn't stop at 10:00 p.m.; they didn't give up at 11:00 p.m.; they praised until their problem crumbled before them.

I want to encourage you to develop a life of praise. Regardless of what you are going through today, find something to praise God for. You may be on top of the world—the kids are getting good grades, your job is not feeling like "work," your spouse is helping out around the house, your health is great, and you found some great sales at the mall—well, *praise God!* Take time to worship God in your quiet time for all of His blessings.

Or you may feel like the world is on top of you—your kids are causing trouble, your job is stressful, your spouse is driving you crazy, you got a bad medical report, and the sales clerk overcharged you—well, *praise God!* Keep worshipping God for His goodness even when it feels like you are in a dark circumstance. Like Paul and Silas, find the good in every situation, and praise God with all of your heart. Your praise is the path to your victory.

I will praise you as long as I live, and in your name I will lift up my hands. (Psalm 63:4 NIV)

3. Let God Take Over The Construction Project

Sometimes, it seems the life we've built, or neglected to build, limits our potential. We made a mess last year, last month, or last week, so we feel we have to suffer the consequences today. This leads to a feeling of hopelessness as we assume that nothing is going to change. I meet a lot of people who are in this situation, and they think the answer to their problem is to try harder. They know what they've built is unstable, but instead of stopping and seeking direction from the Lord, they just keep following their own plans. They're like a homebuilder who starts on the second floor while the first floor is still incomplete.

If you are frustrated with your own efforts and feel you need direction, I suggest you turn the construction project over to God. Study God's Word, spend time in prayer, learn to listen to His voice, and do what He says. Trust that God is good and that He has a good plan for you, and be willing to obey even if He says to stop what you're doing or tells you to do it differently. If you're struggling in your marriage, God may ask *you* to change...even though you want your spouse to change. If you're having financial difficulties, God may tell you to spend less...even though you want Him to give you more. If you're tired and moody, God may tell you to change your diet and get more rest...even though you like your sweets and a hectic schedule.

The point is this: If you'll turn the construction of your life over to God, He'll build something beautiful. It's no accident that Jesus was a carpenter—God is a master builder. He designed the ark, the Tabernacle, the Temple, and the early Church. He wants to design and build your life too. But He's not going to forcefully take the construction away from you—He wants you to give it to Him.

> *If you'll turn the construction of your life over to God, He'll build something beautiful.*

Except the Lord builds the house, they labor in vain who build it; except the Lord keeps the city, the watchman wakes but in vain. (Psalm 127:1)

4. Understand That Your History Is Not Your Destiny

I love what Lamentations 3:23 says about the mercy of God in our lives. In this Scripture, Jeremiah says God's mercies are new and fresh every morning. What a beautiful picture! Just as surely as the sun rose to chase darkness from the horizon today, the grace and mercy of God will rise to chase away any darkness in our own lives. Each day is new and different, filled with a fresh batch of mercy and grace from God.

As long as you think tomorrow is dependent on yesterday, your future will never be different from your past. God sends His mercies fresh each morning, but you have to receive them. The best thing you can do about yesterday is to forget it. Whether you succeeded or failed, it's over. It's time to look ahead.

Who has prepared and done this, calling forth and guiding the destinies of the generations [of the nations] from the beginning? I, the Lord—the first [existing before history began] and with the last [an ever-present, unchanging God]—I am He. (Isaiah 41:4)

I came across a powerful story about a person who overcame obstacles to find a different life in God. I think it will encourage you.

Steven Lavaggi was a graphic artist with tons of talent and plenty of potential. His life was pretty normal by most standards. He was married, had a child, and was working to build his career and a life for his family. That was before things fell apart. One day, Steven's wife unexpectedly left him for a Rolling Stone magazine writer. Steven was left to raise their son alone. This became even more of a challenge when, just 10 days after his wife left, their son was diagnosed with juvenile diabetes. It wasn't too long before Steven lost his graphic arts business, and his life was in total despair.

With trouble swirling around him, Steven turned to God for answers. He was abandoned, broke, and filled with worry; this was a situation only God could repair. So one night, sitting on his bedroom floor, he began searching the Bible for answers. As he read about God's love and the gift of Jesus, the Bible came alive to him. He was forever changed. In that moment, on the cold, wooden floor of his bedroom, Steven Lavaggi gave his life to God.

While seeking God's plan for his life, he developed a passion to create hope for those around him. Since he lived without hope for a season, he knew how powerful hope could be when it came flooding in. After reading Psalm 91:11 ("For He will give His angels [especial] charge over you to accompany and defend and preserve you in all your ways [of obedience and service]"), he used his talents to paint an angel. When a friend encouraged him to make the angel three-dimensional, he worked with a sculptor to cast the image.

The first editions of those sculptures became an instant sensation, but God had an even greater purpose for the angel. Later, while speaking in Soweto, South Africa, as a guest of Parliament; Steven held up one of the angels over his head for the crowd of 3,500 people to see. It happened to have a black patina finish. When he held that sculpture up, the audience jumped to their feet, erupting in joy. A man onstage told him that just a few days before, a preacher had declared, "One of the things we need is for international artists to express the love of God through art, perhaps even painting angels in black."

When he heard this, Lavaggi grabbed a white angel, held it above his head, and said, "These angels were created to be like brothers and sisters, as we are supposed to be." Later, as he thought about that moment, he decided to call the sculptures The Angels of Reconciliation. *That set of angels sold on auction in Cape Town and were presented as a gift to Nelson Mandela. Today, Steven is known as the "Artist of Hope," and his work is seen all over the world.*

Steven Lavaggi's early personal disappointments were turned into eternal triumphs. Though he faced tough days, God was sending away the accusers, breaking down the prison, and building a new life. His new day was different from his old dilemma because he made up his mind to do something new for God.

There is a message for us in Steven's story. When tough days start to pile up, when bad reports start to pour in, and when you begin to wonder if this is the new normal for your life, remember that today can be different. Make up your mind to live differently; praise your way to victory; give God the construction project; and understand that your history is not your destiny. When you do, you'll discover something new. Your life will be more than a casual anecdote. It will be the heroic, dramatic, lifesaving encounter with the living God that will give you hope and enthusiasm for every day.

Summary:

- It's never too late, because Jesus loves to make things new.
- With the help of the Lord, you can make up your mind to live differently.
- Praise is a path to victory.
- When you turn the construction of your life over to God, He builds something beautiful.
- Yesterday doesn't define you. God's mercies are fresh and new every morning.

> *"This new day is too dear, with its hopes and invitations, to waste a moment on the yesterdays."*
>
> —Ralph Waldo Emerson

CHAPTER 3

Getting Past Your Past

"You can't start the next chapter of your life if you keep rereading the last one."

—Anonymous

On July 23, 1996, with the Cold War still in the national consciousness and the eyes of the world upon her, 19-year-old Olympian Kerri Strug stood center stage. The U.S. women's gymnastics program had never before won a team gold medal, but if Strug could put up a near-perfect score in this last event, her team, known as the "Magnificent Seven," would do the impossible: take home a gold medal, beating the talented Russian team.

Television cameras from around the world zoomed in on the face of the gymnast from Tucson, Arizona, as she stared down the only apparatus left between her and history—the infamous vault. Strug blocked out the throbbing pain from her badly injured left ankle, thinking only of the words her coach had just told her: "Kerri, we need you to go one more time. We need you one more time for the gold." The pain was intense, but she was determined to overcome it. After all, Kerri Strug had overcome pain before.

Two years earlier, in a preliminary competition for Nationals, Kerri fell violently while competing on the uneven bars. Her backward fall from the highest bar almost broke her back. The pain was so severe she writhed on the mat crying, "Help. Please. Help me.

Please, Lord." As the medical team attended to her, many thought Kerri's career was over. In the months to come, as she went about the difficult task of rehabilitating her badly sprained back, doubts abounded. Even *if* she could come back physically from the injury, would she ever be the same again mentally? Would she ever be able to get past such a traumatic fall?

In these 1996 Olympics, just 24 months later, she was ready to answer those doubts as she began to run toward the vault with the hopes of a nation on her shoulders. She performed a vault so perfect the Atlanta crowd knew the second she stuck the landing that the Americans had won gold. They went wild, ecstatic they had just witnessed history.

The pictures of Kerri Strug standing on one leg before the judges, and being carried by her coach to the medal stand, are still some of the most inspiring images in U.S. Olympic history. But none of it would have been possible if Kerri Strug had let her past hold her back.

The Key To Your Victory

I believe that God has a gold medal story for each of us. He desires for you to enjoy a life that overcomes obstacles and seizes opportunities. Hebrews 12:1 says that your life is like a race, and that you are "surrounded by so great a cloud of witnesses." I believe these witnesses are cheering for you as you run your race, just waiting to go wild over your triumph in Christ.

But there is an essential key to victory: You have to move past your past. This is so important. There are many people who aren't experiencing victory today because they are focused on yesterday. They spend their days reliving old pain. They are bitter and resentful, stuck in a prison

> *There are many people who aren't experiencing victory today because they are focused on yesterday.*

of pain or disappointment. When they close their eyes, they don't see their dreams for tomorrow; they only see the devastation of yesterday. In other words, an old fall is keeping them from a new victory.

If you are going to experience new victories in God, you are going to have to let go of the past.

- If you're going to see God do new things in your marriage, you'll have to forget some old pains.
- If you're going to have new victory in your health, you'll have to change some past behaviors that are unhealthy.
- If you're going to experience new joy, you'll have to cast those old cares and anxieties on the Lord.
- If you're going to go to a new level in God, you'll have to forgive those people who hurt you in your past.

Had the apostle Paul chosen to live in the past, he never would have accomplished as much for God as he did. We usually think of Paul's great triumphs, but there were many things in his past that he had to overcome.

Before Paul (then known as Saul) was confronted by Jesus on the Damascus Road, he persecuted the early Church. His job was to hunt down and imprison Christians. Acts 7:58 records that Paul stood by as Stephen was stoned, even holding the coats of the men who stoned him.

Of course, Paul was later powerfully saved, but he soon discovered that the disciples were skeptical of his conversion. They didn't want much to do with him. Barnabas was the only one to stand up and vouch for him. It's also important to note that Paul was greatly persecuted for his faith. He didn't always preach to appreciative crowds. On more than one occasion, he was imprisoned, beaten, and even left for dead outside the city gates.

Paul could have let his past keep him from his future. Imagine if he had thought, "Oh, God could never use me! I have made too many mistakes. I persecuted His Church," or "No one believes in me. Even the disciples don't trust me. How can I ever accomplish anything?" or "I can't believe they tried to kill me. I'll never trust people again!"

Aren't you glad he didn't say those things? Paul chose to do what we need to do: move past the past. Listen to his words in Philippians 3:13–14:

> ...*One thing I do [it is my one aspiration]: forgetting what lies behind and straining forward to what lies ahead, I press on toward the goal to win the [supreme and heavenly] prize to which God in Christ Jesus is calling us upward.*

Paul learned the power of overcoming his past. He made it his aim—his *"one aspiration"*—to forget what was behind him, and God used him mightily. I wonder what would happen in your life if you made it your one aspiration to move past your past. Just imagine what God could do in your life if you stopped focusing on the events of yesterday. I believe He would totally revolutionize every area of your life.

Here are three things God has taught me about getting past your past:

1. Forgive Those Who Hurt You

I know what it's like to experience hurt in this life. When I was a young girl, my father sexually abused me, and it took many years for me to receive healing and get to a place where I could forgive him. It just didn't seem fair for me to forgive him when I was the one who had been hurt. But God showed me that holding on to those feelings of bitterness and unforgiveness wasn't hurting him—it was only hurting me.

Unresolved bitterness is an anchor that doesn't just hold you back, it drags you down. It causes you to stay in the past, reliving that hurt every day, pulling you farther and farther from God. The longer you hold on to that abuse, betrayal, rejection, or injustice, the farther you'll be from your destiny.

When you forgive, you allow God to deal with the person who hurt you. You remove yourself from the position of judge (a position that wasn't meant for you anyway), and you let God handle the sin that was perpetrated against you. You'll be amazed at how much better you'll feel—physically, emotionally, and spiritually—when you choose to let go of the bitterness of unforgiveness. Don't think about how unfair it is; just do it because God has asked you to, and because you trust Him and His ways.

Notice I said, "when you choose to let go" of bitterness. Forgiveness is a choice. It doesn't happen accidentally. You must decide that you are going to resist the devil's attempts to keep you living in past hurt and then depend on the power of the Holy Spirit to help you as you strive to be obedient to God's Word. Forgiving the person who hurt you is a choice, an act of obedience to God. When you take this step of faith and choose to forgive, it's like waking up to a brand-new life.

2. Let Go Of Your Past Mistakes

Do you know what God does with the sins and mistakes of your past? He forgets them! Hebrews 8:12 says that God remembers your sins no more. His forgiveness is a free gift, and it is available all the time. I urge you to stop remembering what God has forgotten.

It doesn't matter how hard you try, you are going to make mistakes; we all do. Mistakes are a part of life. How you respond to those mistakes is important in order for you to begin again. That doesn't mean that you don't try to make right decisions and honor God in every part of your life; it just means that you don't dwell on everything you did that was wrong. Beating yourself up over your sins and the mistakes of the past will keep you from believing God for your future. Guilt is energy draining; it weakens us and literally draws us back to the same bad behavior we desire to be free from.

Too many Christians have a "worm mentality." They go around saying, "Woe is me. I'm a sinner. I'm a lowly worm." But that is not what the Word says about you. The Word of God says you are the very righteousness of God in Christ Jesus (2 Corinthians 5:21). What are you going to believe: your shame or your Bible? I pray you'll choose to believe your Bible. The mistakes of your past don't define you; God's Word does.

Refuse to spend your days focused on your mistakes. Don't sit around thinking and talking about past failures. Let them go, and allow God to bring beauty from those ashes. Take hope in the knowledge that God redeems every situation. He can use the mistakes of your past to prepare you for your future. The mistakes you made, the lessons you learned, the forgiveness you received—God can use it all to prepare you for an amazing life in Him.

> *The mistakes you made, the lessons you learned, the forgiveness you received—God can use it all to prepare you for an amazing life in Him.*

3. Don't Live In Your Past Successes

Many people try to fight new battles with old battle plans. They've had successes in their past, so when faced with a new challenge, they assume they can be victorious by responding the same way they did last week, last month, or last year. Instead of seeking God to see what He wants to do in this new day, they try to relive what He did the last time. This connection to the previous "glory days" keeps them tied to the past, missing out on a fresh, new thing God wants to do in this present day.

It's so easy to get comfortable, celebrating the practices of the past. When someone asks why you do something, the answer is often the same: "Because that's how we've always done it!" I've heard this response from individuals, organizations, and even churches. But you need to realize that the wins of the past can be just as dangerous as the losses. Anything that puts your focus on what *used to be* instead of what *can be* will keep you from God's best.

God is always giving His people new strategies. In 2 Samuel 5, God instructed David to attack the Philistines directly; David obeyed and the Israelites won a great victory. In the next verses, the Philistine armies regrouped and once again came against God's people. Instead of assuming the strategies of the past would work, David inquired of the Lord again. This time God said, "Don't attack the same way you did last time," and He gave David a new battle strategy. Once again, the battle was won! The outcome was the same, but the outworking was different.

I believe that God wants you to trust Him for a new battle strategy. If you're frustrated today because the old methods aren't working in your marriage, your family, your finances, your career, or your ministry, do what David did—ask God to give you a new plan. It's great to draw strength from past victories, but God wants you to draw close to Him, believing for the fresh, new thing He wants to do in the present. Even if God instructs us to do the same thing we did the last time, it still needs a fresh anointing that comes through seeking God at the beginning of every venture.

You're A New Person In Christ

As you study the life of Paul, you see that he put all three of those steps into practice on a regular basis. He wrote about forgiveness, he refused to dwell on his past sins, and he trusted in the Lord daily for new direction.

Paul was able to live this way because he discovered it was never too late to begin again. He was a new person in Christ. Paul wasn't a product of his past; he was made new by grace. Look at what he says in Galatians 2:20:

> ...It is no longer I who live, but Christ (the Messiah) lives in me; and the life I now live in the body I live by faith in (by adherence to and reliance on and complete trust in) the Son of God, Who loved me and gave Himself up for me.

Those are the words of a believer who is celebrating the death of his former life. Paul is saying, "I have a new life in Christ. I'm no longer that person I used to be. God has something great for my future." Because Paul chose to live a new life in Christ, his past could no longer hold him back.

When I think about Paul discovering his identity in Christ, I'm reminded of a story I read about a young man who faced a difficult challenge:

> Years ago, in the hills of Tennessee, a baby boy was born to a young, unwed mother. In those days, and in that part of the country, it was scandalous to be an illegitimate child. This young boy grew up never knowing his father and receiving much ridicule in the local community. He was never in public without being painfully aware that he had no father.
>
> One Sunday, when he was about 10 years old, he went to church. He heard there was a new pastor in town, and he was curious to hear this preacher speak. He arrived at church late and planned to sneak out early. This was his usual custom when he went to church; it was just easier to hide than face any embarrassing questions about his family. But this Sunday, the preacher said the benediction so quickly the young boy got caught in the crowd and had to walk out with everyone else.

Just about the time he reached the exit, he felt a large hand on his shoulder. He turned to see the preacher smiling down on him. In a booming voice the preacher asked, "Who are you, son? Whose boy are you?" With every eye in the church staring at him, the boy felt the weight of that old shame settle on his shoulders. Even the preacher would label him as "illegitimate." He froze, not knowing how to answer the question people had asked his entire life: "Who are you, son? Whose boy are you?"

In that instant of silent hesitation, with the entire church looking on, the new preacher studied the face of the boy, and he nodded with a knowing smile. Sensing the moment, he declared, "Wait a minute. I know who you are. I can see the family resemblance. You are a son of God." Patting the boy on the shoulder, the new preacher continued, "You've got a great inheritance, son. Go claim it!"

Ben Hooper never forgot what the preacher told him that day. Not when he finished high school, not when he graduated from college, and not when he served two terms as the governor of Tennessee. Ben loved to tell people the story about his new identity: a child of God.

Though the details are different, your story is very similar to Ben's story . . . and my story . . . and even the apostle Paul's story. God beautifully redeemed you from your past. You are no longer defined by what you did or what someone did to you. God has taken care of your past, and a wonderful future awaits you.

He is rewriting your story and reshaping your identity. In God's narrative, the overlooked become kings, prostitutes become heroes, and persecutors become apostles.

Your new life is in Christ. Your future is bright. Go claim your inheritance!

Summary:

- Victory in the present requires you to move past the past.
- It's time to forgive the person who hurt you. Let God handle it.
- Don't focus on the mistakes of the past. Learn from them and move on.
- Seek God for today's strategy. He has a new plan for your life.
- Never forget: You are a brand-new person in Christ!

Let Go Of The Past

Two friends were talking when one remarked to the other, "Man, you look so depressed. What are you thinking of that could make you so depressed?"

His friend quickly replied, "My future."

"Your future?" his friend asked. "Whatever in the world would make it look so hopeless?" to which his miserable friend sighed and unhappily said, "My past."

"Let the past remain the past. Every day with God is a new day!"

—Joyce

CHAPTER 4

It's Never Too Late

"Start by doing what's necessary; then do what's possible; and suddenly you are doing the impossible."

—Saint Francis of Assisi

These days, cooking shows are extremely popular. Famous chefs and food connoisseurs are in such abundance that we have multiple channels devoted only to cooking. If you are someone who likes to watch these shows, you've probably heard of a show that airs on the Food Network called *Chopped*.

Chopped features different chefs who are competing against one another in a variety of cooking challenges. With each round, the chefs are given a set of ingredients to cook with and a limited amount of time to prepare a dish. At the end of every challenge, you see the chefs dashing madly about the kitchen trying to get their meals on the plate as the show's host dramatically counts down from 10.

10…9…8…7…6…5…4…3…2…1…TIME'S UP!

If a chef doesn't have the dish ready before the time expires, he is usually sent home on the spot. The food may taste great, but it doesn't matter—the chef was too late.

As I think about those chefs running around the kitchen at such a hurried pace, I am thankful that our relationship with God is far different from that picture. God is not rushed or anxious or uptight, and He doesn't want His children to be, either. With God, there are no countdowns, and with God, it is never too late. It's never too late to dream. It's never too late to pray. It's never too late to believe. It's never too late to surrender. And it's *never* too late to begin again.

This is a concept that can be hard for us to grasp in the natural because we live much of our lives fearing the words "too late." If we don't go to college right out of high school, it will be "too late." If we don't get married by a certain age, it will be "too late." If we don't have children before a certain age, it will be "too late." If we don't get promoted in the company faster than another person, or if we don't start putting money toward retirement now, it will be "too late." The list goes on and on.

The truth is we do live in a world that is governed by time, and it's okay to set certain goals and be responsible with the time God gives us; however, when we begin to live hurried, stress-filled lives because we're trying to accomplish our own plans on our own schedule, we are living far short of God's best.

> *When we begin to live hurried, stress-filled lives because we're trying to accomplish our own plans on our own schedule, we are living far short of God's best.*

I believe this is why people grieve over unrealized dreams: because they haven't accomplished what they had planned by a certain age or station in life, they assume the dream is dead. Like any death, the death of a dream brings with it stages of grief. If you've ever had a dream expire, these might seem familiar:

First you're in denial: *I didn't really care about that anyway.*
Then anger: *It isn't fair that others have succeeded and I've failed.*
Then bargaining: *God, if You make this happen, I'll give up fill-in-the-blank.*

Then depression: *I'm a failure. My life is terrible. What a waste.*
And finally acceptance: *Oh, well. It's never going to happen. It's obviously too late.*

Hopes, dreams, plans, and ambitions that operate on your own timetable will always be a source of frustration—there will always be a countdown and a fear of being too late. But those same hopes, dreams, plans, and ambitions submitted to God, and entrusted to His timetable, will always be a source of life... because with God, it is never too late.

Just The Right Time

Sarah was 90 years old when she overheard the Lord tell Abraham that she was going to give birth to a son (Genesis 18). Painfully aware that she was barren and past the age of childbearing, the Bible tells us that Sarah laughed at the thought. Now this wasn't a laugh of joy, but rather a laugh of disbelief. Sarah thought to herself: "At my age? Yeah, right. There's no way!"

It would be easy to categorize Sarah's scoffing as a simple lack of faith, but her response is a little more nuanced than that—this is the response of someone who has grieved the death of her dream.

In her culture, childbearing was what gave a woman significance. If she couldn't have children, she was useless to her husband and useless to her community. So imagine what Sarah has dealt with her entire adult life: her own maternal instincts are unfulfilled, her marriage has endured the strain of infertility, and her significance as a person has been attacked. Undoubtedly, as the years added up and the clock counted down, Sarah took the painful walk through denial, anger, bargaining, and depression. By the time we find her in Genesis chapter 18, she has settled into the acceptance stage—"It's never going to happen; it's simply too late." For Sarah, it was easier to laugh and not get her hopes up than to hope and be disappointed.

Do you know what that feels like? Are you living a life that feels incomplete because something you have desperately longed for hasn't happened? All you wanted was a happy marriage, but he left you. You dreamed your whole life of having a baby, but you haven't conceived. You thought you'd be together forever, but the person you loved has died. You've tried and tried to heal a relationship, but it remains broken. You gave years to a career, but it hasn't panned out. Do you know the grief of living under the burden of "too late"?

If that's you, I want to remind you of something you may have forgotten as you've waited. Your "too late" is God's "just in time." He loves to do things in your life that man assumes are impossible. God's thoughts are not your thoughts, and His ways are not your ways (Isaiah 55:8). In other words, God's timetable is different from your timetable. With Him, there is no such thing as too late. God always shows up at just the right time.

> Your "too late" is God's "just in time."

Some people say that God shows up at the last second, but I don't believe that. I believe God shows up at the perfect second! God is not rushing to beat a deadline. He isn't saying, "Oh, I've got to hurry up. I'm almost out of time!" The opposite is true; He is divinely orchestrating His perfect plan for your life. As you study the Word of God, you see phrases like "*in due time*" (1 Peter 5:6), "*at the appointed time*" (Habakkuk 2:3), and "*at the proper time*" (Galatians 4:4). These phrases describe a Master clock-builder Who accounts for every second and always knows the right thing to do at the right time.

Romans 5:6 says, "You see, at just the right time, when we were still powerless, Christ died for the ungodly" (NIV). Your very salvation was provided through the sacrifice of Jesus in God's perfect timing. Jesus paid for your sins at just the right time. I believe that if God is big enough to provide for our salvation in His perfect timing, He can provide for our daily lives in that same perfection.

Is Anything Too Hard Or Too Wonderful For The Lord?

When Sarah laughed at the thought of having a baby in her old age, God asked a powerful question: "Why did Sarah laugh, saying, Shall I really bear a child when I am so old? Is anything too hard or too wonderful for the Lord?" (Genesis 18:13–14).

God is asking, "Sarah, why are you seeing life according to your timetable? Why have you doubted My promise? Don't you know that it's never too late when you submit your life to Me?" I believe God is asking you the same question today: Is anything too hard or too wonderful for the Lord?

Is it too hard or too wonderful for the Lord to...restore that relationship?

> ...give you a family?
> ...heal your pain?
> ...provide the job you need?
> ...answer your prayer?

With God, all things are possible. There is nothing He cannot do. He may do it differently than you planned, and He may do it later than you planned, but His ways and His timing are always better than anything you can imagine. Take a moment to tell God, "Lord, I'm open to whatever You have for me. It may not be what I planned,

> *With God, all things are possible. There is nothing He cannot do.*

and it may not happen on my timetable, but I trust Your perfect plan for my life. I refuse to give up on You, but I choose to give up worry, anxiety, and fear. I know nothing is too hard or too wonderful for You!"

Now be open to new things in your life. God may cause you to conceive a child, or He may call you to adopt. God may heal that broken friendship, or He may give you the strength to leave it behind because it would only cause you more pain. God may bring that spouse back, or He may bring someone new along who will bring even greater joy into your life. God may give you that promotion, or He may have a new career for you. God is full of good ideas, and He wants to share them with you!

My point is this: God may do exactly what you've been dreaming for, or He may do something so great you couldn't have even thought to dream it. I won't pretend to know the details of what God is going to do in your life—I just want to encourage you to be open to His perfect plan that will happen in His perfect timing.

Never Too Late For Success

On September 9, 1890, Harland Sanders was born in the rural, Midwestern town of Henryville, Indiana. Harland's father died when Harland was only six years old, leaving him to watch his two younger siblings each day as his mother returned to the workforce to provide for the family.

By the age of seven, Harland learned the art of cooking as he settled into his role as caregiver for his younger siblings, but this was one of his few early accomplishments. Harland dropped out of school in sixth grade and moved from job to job as a teenager and young adult. He tried his hand at a number of different occupations including farmhand, army mule-tender, motel operator, tire salesman, (unsuccessful) political candidate, and gas station operator.

At the age of 40, Harland was running a service station in Corbin, Kentucky. Though others may have felt sorry for themselves to be stuck working at a service station, Harland used the opportunity to display his home-taught culinary skills and feed hungry travelers. Quick and delicious, Harland's signature dish became the topic of conversation all over the state. Travelers would make Harland's gas station a regular stop so they could enjoy his cooking. He eventually moved his operation out of the service station and started a restaurant across the street. He spent many years in that restaurant perfecting his cooking technique and his special blend of spices. Business was booming, and the locals raved over chicken that was "finger lickin' good." Harland's future finally began to look bright.

However, at the age of 60, Harland was forced to close his restaurant when the state built a new highway where his restaurant was located. It appeared the dream was over. Harland was too old to begin again. How would he respond? It seemed like he was out of options. He was too old. It was too late.

But Harland refused to sit by feeling depressed and sorry for himself. Instead, he acted. Many people might see their first Social Security check as a sign that life is ending; Harland saw it as a sign that life was just beginning. He took that first check of $105 and used it to begin franchising his signature dish: fried chicken. He traveled across the country, frying up chicken for any restaurant that would let him. He negotiated deals that paid him a nickel for every chicken the restaurant sold using his blend of herbs and spices.

In 1964, with over 600 franchised outlets around the country, Harland sold his interest in the company for $2 million to a group of investors. The company went public two years later and was listed on the New York Stock Exchange a few years after that. Harland stayed very involved in the company he founded. He spent the rest of his life traveling 250,000 miles a year visiting his restaurants around the country. He became famous the world over; however, no one called him Harland anymore—they called him Colonel. Colonel Sanders, the face of Kentucky Fried Chicken, knew this one thing about life: it's never too late to begin again.

Take A Step

Harland Sanders's story is an inspiration to anyone who ever felt like it is too late for them to do something. If he could accomplish all of that with the power of his own determination, just imagine what you can do with the power of God at your disposal. The possibilities are endless.

Today, I want you to make the decision to do whatever God leads you to do. You may not have all the answers, and you may not know every step to take, but by faith, I want you to take the first step. You've grieved long enough. Now it's time to believe! And an important part of believing is taking an action step. Maybe that first step is:

- Applying for a class at your local community college.
- Forgiving the person you've been holding a grudge against.
- Going to church for the first time in years.
- Making an appointment with a nutritionist.
- Sending out a resume.
- Calling an adoption agency.
- Applying for the promotion at work that you would love to have.
- Confronting the problem in your marriage instead of ignoring it.
- Daring to pray bold prayers, asking God for what seems impossible.

If you're familiar with the Bible, you know that God kept His promise to Abraham and Sarah. He told them, "At the appointed time, when the season [for her delivery] comes around, I will return to you and Sarah shall have borne a son" (Genesis 18:14). And the fulfillment of God's promise was greater than anything Sarah could have imagined. She hoped for a child; God gave her a child and so much more—she and Abraham were the parents of a nation.

If you've found yourself laughing at the thought of your dream coming true, I dare you to hope again. God's appointed time hasn't passed. His promise is still true. He's right on time.

Summary:

- God's timetable is different from your timetable.
- Just because it hasn't happened yet doesn't mean it won't.
- God always does things in His perfect timing.
- Be open to the fact that God may answer your prayer in a way you never thought possible.
- An important part of believing is taking an action step.
- Be at peace and enjoy life while you wait.

Finding Peace In The Waiting

I didn't even start the ministry that I have now until I was 42 years old. I had been teaching the Bible for 10 years before that—five years in home Bible studies and five years in someone else's ministry—but I didn't start our ministry until I was 42. I want to encourage you to trust that when God gets you where He wants you to be, and He gets you in the condition He wants you to be in, He can fast-track your success! It's unbelievable what God has done in our ministry and the number of people He has allowed us to reach since we started *Joyce Meyer Ministries.*

Just because you're 30 (or 40 or 50 or whatever) and you don't know yet what God is going to do with you . . . it's not over! We must refuse to live our lives trying to figure everything out all of the time. I've learned this firsthand. I can tell you that I just about drove myself crazy trying to figure everything out in the early years of the ministry. I thought I just *had* to know how things were going to work out. I worried, reasoned, and wondered all day every day, and it was useless.

God wanted me to trust Him, and that is what He wants you to do also. When God's time was right for me, He gave me what I call a "suddenly." Something I had desired for years and had been unsuccessful in accomplishing SUDDENLY happened by the grace of God. Our ministry started growing at an amazing pace, and we had the opportunity to help millions of people around the world. My dream was coming true beyond my wildest imagination!

Sadly, I had forfeited my peace and joy through worrying about things that I could not change and trying to make things happen that only God could make happen.

My husband, Dave, found it easy to trust God. He would simply cast his care and say that God would take care of it. God always did take care of things eventually, and Dave enjoyed his life while waiting, but I wasted mine being miserable.

God's Word says,

Peace I leave with you; My [own] peace I now give and bequeath to you. Not as the world gives do I give to you. Do not let your hearts be troubled, neither let them be afraid. [Stop allowing yourselves to be agitated and disturbed; and do not permit yourselves to be fearful and intimidated and cowardly and unsettled.] (John 14:27)

You can choose peace. You don't have to allow yourself to be agitated and disturbed. Isn't that good news? I want to encourage you: Whatever you're waiting for today, choose to live in peace. God is going to bring His perfect plan to pass in your life. It's never too late for His plan . . . and it's never too late for His peace.

CHAPTER 5

All You Need Is A Moment

"How wonderful it is that nobody need wait a single moment before beginning to improve the world."

—Anne Frank

Before February 15, 2006, very few people outside of the small town of Greece, New York, had ever heard of Jason McElwain. Today, his story inspires millions around the world. And it all started on a cold winter night in an overcrowded high school gymnasium. He had a moment no one in attendance would ever forget.

Jason was born to David and Debbie McElwain in this small, western New York town on October 1, 1987. At a very early age, Jason was diagnosed with autism, a developmental disorder that affects the brain's normal development of social and communication skills. As you might imagine, Jason's parents were worried he might never lead a normal life.

Throughout his childhood, Jason worked to overcome his disability. In time, he learned how to interact with other children, developing social skills so he could play with classmates and have friends just like every other boy and girl. As hard as autism tried, it couldn't keep Jason down.

In high school, Jason failed to make the varsity basketball team, but he didn't let that keep him down, either. If he couldn't be a player, he would be the team manager, a responsibility he didn't take lightly. Jason showed up for every game, handing out towels and water bottles while wearing the shirt and tie of a team manager. Though he enjoyed helping the team, his real dream was to one day wear a uniform and maybe even get in a game.

On February 15, the student body of Greece Athena High School crowded into the gymnasium excited for the evening basketball game, but no one was more excited than Jason. Earlier in the day, his coach, Jim Johnson, asked Jason if he would like to trade his shirt and tie for a team uniform. (Tonight was the last home game of the season, and Coach Johnson wanted Jason to wear a jersey like every other boy on the team.) Though he had no promise that he would actually get in the game, Jason excitedly dressed out and joined his teammates on the bench. He felt like one of the guys.

In the fourth quarter, with just four minutes left in the game, Coach Johnson did the unexpected. He looked down the bench and motioned for Jason to check in. Jason couldn't believe it. He thought, "Is this actually happening?" Time seemed to move in slow motion as Jason got up from the bench and entered the game. Neither he nor anyone in attendance that night could have foreseen what would happen next—they were about to experience the power of a moment.

The students and parents in attendance cheered wildly for Jason as he stepped onto the court. Everyone was happy that he was getting a chance to play, and they all hoped that he might even make a shot. Even Coach Johnson prayed, "God, just let him make a basket."

With the game winding down, and the crowd on the edge of their seats, Jason received a pass from a teammate. He turned around and did what he had dreamed of doing his whole life: shot a three-pointer. Pandemonium ripped through the gym as the unthinkable happened... *SWISH!* Every student, parent, and player jumped up and down for joy, screaming cheers for their friend who had overcome so much in his life. Jason made a basket in the last game of the season! What an incredible story. But Jason wasn't finished.

With each trip down the court, Jason turned and shot again. *SWISH! SWISH! SWISH! SWISH!* Shot after shot poured through the basket. And with every new three-pointer made, the crowd jumped higher and screamed louder than before. As time expired, Jason released one last shot from an impossibly far distance, and yes, once again, the ball swished through the net. The entire student body of Greece Athena High School rushed the court to hug Jason. He scored six three-point baskets in the last four minutes of the game, becoming the team's high scorer. Jason McElwain, the boy with autism, was carried around the gym on the shoulders of his friends. Together, they celebrated the greatest moment they had ever been a part of.

Someone in the crowd captured Jason's performance on video that night, and the story went viral. Every major news organization ran with the video. Hollywood quickly bought the rights to make a movie out of it. Athletes, celebrities, and even President George W. Bush came to meet Jason. But better than all of that, Jason's story became an inspiration for people around the world afflicted with autism. Jason's life changed on one special night—Jason's life changed in one powerful moment.

The Power Of A Moment

I want to close out section one of this book by talking about the power of a moment—what God can do *suddenly*. During my years in ministry, I've met many people who have lost hope. Their lives feel broken and damaged beyond repair. They love the Lord, but they think that somehow their chance to live out His plan is over. The idea of getting their lives back on track is just too intimidating of a process. To further complicate their situation, the devil attacks, telling them they are worthless and God won't use them.

You may know someone who feels this way; you may feel this way yourself. Overlooked, disqualified, forgotten. It can be pretty discouraging to be the person handing out towels while everyone around you seems to be getting in the game.

But as a child of God, there is something especially encouraging you need to remember today: *God can do more in one moment than you can do in a lifetime.* There is no situation that intimidates Him. There is no mess, no dysfunction, no abuse, no pain that He can't heal. One word from God, one moment in His presence, can change the entire course of your life.

> God can do more in one moment than you can do in a lifetime.

As I study the Word of God, I am amazed to see how people's lives are changed in just one moment. On nearly every page, men and women of the Bible have powerful encounters with God that result in instant and immediate life changes. Lives that seemed to be headed nowhere are suddenly set on a divine course.

Think about David. At the beginning of 1 Samuel chapter 16, he is just a shepherd. He spends his days singing in the fields while watching his father's sheep. But one day, the prophet Samuel shows up at his doorstep and anoints him the next king of Israel. In one day—with one moment—his entire life changed.

Or think about Moses. At the beginning of Exodus chapter 3, he is an outlaw who has spent the last 40 years of his life hiding in Midian. One day he spots a bush that is on fire but doesn't seem to be burning up. God speaks to him from that bush, and Moses walks away from that encounter as the man who will deliver the Hebrew children from bondage in Egypt. In one day—with one moment— his entire life changed.

We see the same thing in the life of Mary; it's a story we retell every Christmas. At the beginning of the book of Luke, Mary is a young virgin pledged to be married. One day, an angel of the Lord shows up and tells her she has found favor with God and she will bear a Son who will deliver the world from their sins. In one day—with one moment—her entire life changed.

I'm amazed when I read about how Jesus called the disciples. They were each going about their daily routines when all of a sudden the Lord shows up and says, "Follow Me." With that one invitation, they leave their old lives behind. In one day—with one moment—their entire lives changed.

These stories, and others like them, send a clear message to every person who feels their life is hopeless: *Your life can change in a moment.* If you'll trust that God has a plan for your life and wait patiently, He'll do more in a minute than you could do in 10 years. Your past, your limitations, your obstacles are no match for the power of God. He spoke the world into existence with the power of His word; He can speak new life into your situation.

> *Your past, your limitations, your obstacles are no match for the power of God.*

Now, I'm not suggesting a "quick-fix" Christian life. What God reveals suddenly, He will often implement gradually. Anyone who has walked with God for any length of time will tell you that serving God isn't about easy answers. If you think God is going to appear like a genie and—*POOF!*—make all of your problems magically disappear, you're going to be disappointed. The Christian life isn't always lived on the mountaintop; there are days you still have to go through the valley. Following God takes determination and discipline.

In each of the stories I mentioned, there was a gradual implementation of the sudden revelation. After David was anointed king, he had to patiently go through the process of becoming a king. Moses didn't lead the people out of Egypt the very next day; he had to trust God and obediently carry out God's plan for his life. Mary had to trust God for the promise to be fulfilled in her life even when she and others didn't fully comprehend what it meant. The disciples faithfully walked with the Lord every day, whether they felt like it or not.

Your life is no different. You will need to get to know God intimately, and that requires regular study of God's Word, spending time in prayer, and choosing to believe God's promises. Let God be part of every facet of your life. There will be days when you don't feel like praying, reading the Word, or serving God, and days when you don't feel God's presence. These are the days when you simply refuse to live controlled by your feelings. Instead, you ask God to help you walk in obedience and submit to His Word whether you feel like it or not. I often say that if we truly desire to live victoriously, then "we must be willing to do what is right when it feels wrong."

But even in the midst of pressing through times that are difficult, the fact remains that God can bring "suddenly" moments to your life. Moments that are so powerful and so miraculous, they change everything. One word from God, one touch from His Spirit, one promise from His Word, being in the right place at the right time, can set your life on a new course. Though things in your life may seem to be unchanging, they can be changed in a moment.

> *A good question to ask yourself is, "What am I expecting?"*

It is important that we live with expectancy. We should expect things to change at any time instead of expecting them to always stay the way they have always been. Living with a "positive expectancy" is a facet of faith, and God's Word says that without faith, it is impossible to please God (Hebrews 11:6). It pleases God when we expect His divine help rather than expecting trouble. A good question to ask yourself is, "What am I expecting?"

Any Time, Any Place

I've had several "suddenly" moments in my life. One of those was when God called me into ministry. There wasn't a gymnasium full of high school students, and no one is making a movie about it, but it was a moment I'll never forget.

I was making my bed one morning, and the voice of the Lord spoke to me and said, *Joyce, you are going to go all over the place and share My Word. You're going to have a large teaching ministry.* It wasn't an audible voice, but it might as well have been; it was *that* clear. God changed my life in a moment. From that day forward, I knew teaching was my destiny, and I've had the overwhelming desire to teach the Word of God ever since.

It's not where you are or what you are doing in the moment that changes you—I was doing the average, ordinary task of making my bed—it's the power of God in that moment that changes you. God can meet you at any time and at any place. You could be at work, out shopping, taking a walk, mowing your grass, in church, talking to a friend, reading your Bible, or even making your bed. When He shows up, your life is "suddenly" changed.

Maybe there have been times while reading the first section of this book that you thought, "That sounds great...for someone else. My problem is too big; my life is beyond help." Maybe you can't even start to fathom how you could begin again in your life. If that's you, I want you to know that God has a moment for you. In fact, it might be right now as you read these words. A spark of faith can fill your heart and enable you to believe that it's not too late to begin again! You don't have to have all the answers, you don't have to figure out how everything is going to work, and you don't have to make it happen yourself. All you have to do is be open to the Lord and listen for His voice.

It is a mistake to think that God can speak to us only when we are doing something we consider to be spiritual. God is with us all the time, in every place. The time or place isn't important, but your level of expectancy is. Dare to believe that God has a great future in store for you and ask Him to reveal it to you.

But watch out. What God reveals in your moment may be bigger than you think. David killed a giant, Moses delivered a nation, Mary gave birth to the Messiah, and the disciples turned the world upside down. God always does more in your life than you could have done by yourself. Get ready! Be excited and realize that today may be the day when everything changes.

Summary:

- One word from God, one moment in His presence, can change the entire course of your life.
- Don't lose hope. God loves to work "suddenly."
- What God reveals in a moment, we walk out daily.
- You will never be disappointed when you decide to seek God.
- Expectancy is key! Live each day expecting to see God work in your life.

Trusting God's Timing—Waiting For Your Moment

For the vision is yet for an appointed time and it hastens to the end [fulfillment]; it will not deceive or disappoint. Though it tarry, wait [earnestly] for it, because it will surely come; it will not be behindhand on its appointed day. (Habakkuk 2:3)

And let us not lose heart and grow weary and faint in acting nobly and doing right, for in due time and at the appointed season we shall reap, if we do not loosen and relax our courage and faint. (Galatians 6:9)

The Lord does not delay and is not tardy or slow about what He promises . . . (2 Peter 3:9)

Wait and hope for and expect the Lord; be brave and of good courage and let your heart be stout and enduring. Yes, wait for and hope for and expect the Lord. (Psalm 27:14)

To everything there is a season, and a time for every matter or purpose under heaven . . . (Ecclesiastes 3:1)

My times are in Your hands; deliver me from the hands of my foes and those who pursue me and persecute me. (Psalm 31:15)

Thus says the Lord, In an acceptable and favorable time I have heard and answered you, and in a day of salvation I have helped you . . . (Isaiah 49:8)

For He says, In the time of favor (of an assured welcome) I have listened to and heeded your call, and I have helped you on the day of deliverance (the day of salvation). Behold, now is truly the time for a gracious welcome and acceptance [of you from God]; behold, now is the day of salvation! (2 Corinthians 6:2)

IT'S NEVER TOO LATE TO...

- ✓ *Start Over*
- ✓ *Chase Your Dreams*
- ✓ *Create Healthy Relationships*
- ✓ *Understand God's Power*
- ✓ *Change Your Ways*
- ✓ *Be Positive*
- ✓ *Hope*
- ✓ *Accept The Lord*
- ✓ *Make A Difference*
- ✓ *Forgive The Person Who Hurt You*
- ✓ *Learn Something New*
- ✓ *Do What You've Always Wanted To Do*
- ✓ *Say "I'm Sorry"*
- ✓ *Be Inspired*
- ✓ *Begin Again*
- ✓ *Put Your Past In Your Past*

PART II

What's Stopping You?

...the old [previous moral and spiritual condition] has passed away....

2 Corinthians 5:17; Part II

CHAPTER 6

Did You Pay For That?

"Jesus paid it all. All to Him I owe. Sin had left a crimson stain. He washed it white as snow."

—Elvina M. Hall

Sometimes God will speak to us through the everyday events of life. He can use the beauty of a sunset, a conversation with a friend, or a random experience to show us a truth from His Word. I've had this happen in my life many times, but I want to share one specific event.

I went to a local mall to buy a purse I'd had my eye on for a while. I made my purchase and the sales clerk put the purse in a bag, along with my receipt. As I was exiting the store, the sensor at the door started beeping loudly. The sales clerk must have left a tag on the purse because it set off the shoplifting alarm. An employee came rushing over, and my first thought was, "I hope they don't think I'm trying to steal something." No one was rude to me, but they gave me a look as if to say, "Did you pay for that?!?!" Thankfully, I had my receipt in the bag and was able to prove that everything in the bag was mine. I was slightly embarrassed, but I didn't feel guilty. After all, everything had already been paid for.

What happened that day is a good picture of what often happens in the spiritual realm. There are times in the life of every believer when you are faced with the question, *Did you pay for that?* When

God gives you a new beginning, there will always be skeptics who doubt you deserve it. For reasons that I'll talk about in the next few pages, people will shake their heads in disapproval, wondering: "Do you deserve a new chance? Have you earned a better future? Should you really get to be this happy?" All these questions are part of a larger spiritual question: "Did you pay for that?!?!"

The truth is, you didn't pay for it…and neither did I. You don't deserve it, and neither do I. But this is what makes the Gospel story so beautiful. The Bible tells us that Jesus paid the price so we could receive God's goodness! He paid for our sin when we could not, and His sacrifice at Calvary was a once-and-for-all payment. Every sin, every mistake, every dysfunction, every bad decision—He paid for them all.

Not only has your past been paid for, your future has been pro-

> *Not only has your past been paid for, your future has been provided for.*

vided for. Out of His great love for you, God has provided everything you need to live an overcoming, abundant, joy-filled life. That's why a fresh start in life is such a powerful promise. It's not anything you've earned; it is a gift from God. That's good news!

Changing Buses

When you start pursuing God on a deeper level, not everyone will be happy about it. There are people in your life who want you to be just as emotionally unhealthy, miserable, and unhappy as they are. It's like the old expression, "Misery loves company." When you start making changes in your life in obedience to God's Word, be prepared to face some resistance.

Think of it like riding a bus. You are deciding to change the direction of your life in certain areas—to begin again. So in order to change direction, you are getting off the old bus and getting on a new bus going a different way. That's great for you, but your friends are on the old bus. They might not like the fact that you're leaving. "Hey, hold on! Where do you think you're going? We were supposed to be on this bus together."

Sadly, many people will try to keep you on the bus with them. This shows up in a number of ways:

- They may continue to tempt you with old behaviors.
- They may refuse to respect your new convictions.
- They may try to make you feel guilty for improving your life.
- They may constantly create a negative environment that makes it difficult for you to live for God.
- They may make you feel like it's too late to start over.

Have you ever noticed that some of the most difficult resistance can come from the people closest to you? Longtime friends, trusted colleagues, and even family members can be the first people to discourage you when you begin to tell them about the decisions you're making for God. I'm not saying these are bad people, but they can be a bad influence in your life if you allow them to hold you back from God's best. Sadly, if people aren't ready to move on themselves, they often try to hold us back in order to feel better about their own lack of initiative.

Don't let others keep you from receiving the new things God has for you. Their alarms of accusation are no match for the grace of God. Whatever you are after today—new health, a new mind-set, a new attitude, a new relationship, a new boldness, or a new career— remember, it has all been paid for. In fact, your entire life was paid for by the sacrifice of Jesus. First Corinthians 7:23 says:

> *You were bought with a price [purchased with a preciousness and paid for by Christ]; then do not yield yourselves up to become [in your own estimation] slaves to men [but consider yourselves slaves to Christ].*

I love how the *Message* version articulates that verse. It says:

> *...A huge sum was paid out for your ransom. So please don't, out of old habit, slip back into being or doing what everyone else tells you. Friends, stay where you were called to be. God is there. Hold the high ground with him at your side.*

You can only "hold the high ground with him at your side" if you choose to live for God rather than other people. He should be the only person you are trying to please. If those around you are keeping you from taking a new direction, you need to confront those people in love and explain to them that their actions are hurting you.

If they don't receive that, I would encourage you to pray and ask God what to do next. If it is a friend or a business associate, He may tell you to set that relationship aside. It doesn't mean that you don't love that person; it just means that you may need to limit the influence they have over you. When God called me to teach His Word, the people who tried to hold me back were church friends. They were not mean people, they just didn't understand my new direction, and as a result, they felt threatened by it. People usually critically judge, or even reject, what they don't understand.

You may experience some rejection in order to get off the old bus and get on a new one. Your new life will be wonderful, but there may be those who will either not understand, or who will be jealous. Be determined to follow God, because with Him, you will always end up in the right place with the best life!

I read that Henry Ford once said, "My best friend is the one who brings out the best in me." I believe that is especially true in the life of a believer, considering the best in you is the Spirit of God. A true friend is going to encourage you to follow God's direction, not act as a hindrance as you seek God's best for your life.

Hebrews 12:1 (NIV) says to "throw off everything that hinders" in order to run the race God has set for you.

Here are some things that can hinder your walk with God...

1. The Negative Attitude Of Others

You don't have to sit around and listen to friends or coworkers murmur and complain all day. If you stay in that environment, it is going to affect your spirit. You may not be able to avoid them every second of the day, but you can limit the access they have to you. Maybe you need to listen to part of a good teaching during your break. Or maybe you need to take a walk and fellowship with God during your lunch rather than join a negative conversation.

Another thing you can do is change the direction of the conversation. If those around you are griping and complaining about their job, why don't you say, "Well, I don't know about you, but I'm just thankful I *have* a job today. It might not be perfect, but it's better than nothing." You might be surprised at how your positive words can influence others.

The most important thing is to realize that negative words can affect your spirit. Don't allow the negativity of those around you to pull you down and take your focus away from the Lord. Fill your life with positive things that build you up and increase your joy.

> *Don't allow the negativity of those around you to pull you down and take your focus away from the Lord.*

2. The Impossible Expectations Of Others

Yes, it's important to find time to help others and serve those around you, but you can't live your entire life trying to impress or please others. I've discovered no matter how hard you try, for some people, it will never be enough. There are some people who are going to expect you to do more and more until you reach a breaking point. Sadly, there are people who will use you for their own benefit, or even misuse or abuse you. You must be responsible to protect yourself and learn to say "no" when you know that you need to.

One of the most important things you can do in life is let go of your need to please people. Trying to please others and trying to meet their expectations will cause you to live the life *they* want you to live and miss the life that God wants you to live. There is no joy in that, only bondage.

Rather than trying to please others, live your life to please God. Colossians 1:10 says: "That you may walk (live and conduct yourselves) in a manner worthy of the Lord, fully pleasing to Him and desiring to please Him in all things." This is where you will find rest and peace for your soul. If you want to experience the life-changing joy of the Lord, let go of the unrealistic expectations of others and live for God each day.

3. Jealousy Of Others

Not everyone is going to be happy when you begin a new life in God. Your new attitude, new mind-set, and new level of joy can cause others to be jealous of the things they are lacking in their own lives.

As you begin to walk closer to God, you will experience a new level of blessing in your life, and there will be some folks who are jealous of what God has given you. A friend of mine was never able to fully rejoice with me when God blessed me. When she discovered that God had done something special for me, her comment was always, "It must be nice; I am waiting for things like that to happen to me." Her tone and facial expression, as well as her words, let me know that she was jealous, and it made me not want to be her friend.

And it's not just material things. As you follow God, there will be people who are jealous of your newfound peace, emotional health, or joyful outlook on life. You used to be anxious and stressed-out all the time, but now you are casting your cares on God and living in a new level of rest. There will be people who are envious of what you have found.

Don't apologize for what God has given you just because someone else is jealous of it. If they can't be happy for you, then they have some issues they need to get right with God. You can encourage them and pray for them, but don't let their jealousy discourage you. Rejoice in the blessings of the Lord!

Don't let the accusations of suspicious people intimidate you into giving up what God has provided. It's true: You didn't pay for the grace of God in your life, but you didn't have to. God loved you so much He sent Jesus to pay the price for you.

> God loved you so much He sent Jesus to pay the price for you.

Everything in your life can be restored—*it's never too late!* Mary and Martha thought it was too late for Jesus to help Lazarus. He had been dead for four days and was beginning to rot by the time Jesus showed up, but he was raised from the dead by the power of God. I think it is safe to say that Lazarus got a fresh start.

You can have a great marriage—*it's never too late!* You can be the kind of parent you've always wanted to be—*it's never too late!* You can get out of debt—*it's never too late!* You can evict worry and anxiety from your home—*it's never too late!* You can establish healthy, life-giving habits as a part of your daily routine—*it's never too late!* You can live a beautiful, stress-free, happy life—*it's never too late!*

The Bible is your receipt. All of its amazing promises are yours. It's all been paid for!

Summary:

- Jesus paid the price for your sin. He bought you once and for all!
- Not only has your past been paid for, your future has been provided for.
- Be careful: some of the most difficult resistance can come from the people closest to you.
- Don't allow the negative attitude of others to hold you back.
- Live your life to please God. His opinion is the only one that counts.

"*You have enemies? Good. That means you've stood up for something sometime in your life.*"

—Winston Churchill

CHAPTER 7

Who Do You Think You Are?!?

"You aren't loved because you're valuable. You're valuable because God loves you."

—Anonymous

She was 23 years old when she picked up the phone and dialed the number. In many ways, she dreaded making the call, but running from the dread was no longer an option. It was time for answers.

For years, Nejdra Nance suspected something wasn't right. There were warning signs; there were inconsistencies. But Nejdra brushed away the suspicions and ignored the doubts. The truth was too painful to even consider.

But by winter of 2011, she simply couldn't avoid the mounting evidence any longer: she never felt comfortable around her relatives; she looked nothing like her mother; she had no Social Security card, and had never even seen her birth certificate.

And then there were the photos. Some of the baby photos on the website looked eerily familiar. Nejdra kept going back to the site time and time again, terrified of the implications. It was a website for missing and exploited children.

Finally, she made the call.

When a crisis counselor answered the phone, Nejdra Nance spoke the words that had haunted her for 23 years: "I don't know who I am."

The story that unfolded in the days following that phone call read more like a Hollywood script than reality. As the truth came out, police detectives showed up and international news outlets ran with the unbelievable story of Carlina Renae White: the woman who solved her own kidnapping.

The story began on a warm August night in 1987, when the worried parents of a 19-day-old infant, Carlina Renae White, brought their newborn daughter to a Manhattan hospital with a high fever. Just a few hours later, the unthinkable happened: little Carlina was reported missing from the pediatric ward.

The police immediately focused their investigation on a mysterious woman seen lingering around the hospital in a nurse's uniform, but other than a few eyewitness accounts, they had little to work with. The hospital's surveillance cameras weren't operational that day, and every lead the detectives had eventually grew cold.

Days turned to weeks, weeks turned to months, and months turned to years. The abduction of Carlina Renae White went unsolved.

In the subsequent years, while her parents grieved their loss, her abductor, Ann Pettway, raised Carlina in a small Connecticut town just 45 minutes away. Mentally distraught and desperate for a family, Pettway had posed as a nurse that tragic August night, tucked baby Carlina under her coat, and fled the scene, never to be seen again.

The baby would never be called Carlina by her kidnapper...now the baby girl was Nejdra. And though she was raised in a relatively normal environment, nothing can change the fact that so much had been stolen from her. As a child, she never knew her real parents, her real heritage, or her real identity. She would spend many of her formative years thinking, "I don't know who I am."

The story ends with a measure of justice. After Carlina made that call to the *National Center for Missing and Exploited Children*, the authorities apprehended Ann Pettway, who eventually confessed to her crime. (Pettway is currently serving a jail sentence in a Connecticut prison.)

But Carlina's story is a little more complicated. Yes, she was introduced to her biological parents, and she was glad to get answers to the questions that had nagged her since her teenage years. But once the news crews left and the media circus subsided, Carlina had to go about the difficult process of picking up the pieces of her life.

One of those pieces was her identity. Who was she? What would she call herself: Carlina White or Nejdra Nance? It was a difficult question to answer. When you've been lied to your entire life, the answers aren't as easy as one might think. In an interview with *New York Magazine*, Carlina said that she has moved on with her life, but she doesn't identify with either name, Carlina or Nejdra. Instead, she tells people to call her "Netty."

First Carlina. Then Nejdra. Now Netty.

Identity Crisis

I believe one of the major issues facing the Church today is identity theft. In the new cyber society in which we live, we think of identity theft as a compromised password or a stolen credit card, but I'm talking about something far more dangerous.

I'm talking about people who—like Carlina White—have been lied to for so long, they've begun to believe the lie. They don't know who they are, and they have no idea where they're going. They may even be a believer in Jesus Christ who loves God, but has believed the lies of Satan so long that they simply don't know their tremendous value as a child of God. They either don't know about the rich promises of God to His children, or if they do, they have assumed those promises are for the more "perfect" Christians and don't include them.

Truthfully, many Christians are walking around saying, "I don't know who I am." They are living lives far short of their destinies because they are unaware of their identities.

You need to understand that this identity crisis doesn't happen by accident. It is one of the favorite tricks of the devil. If he can keep you from realizing who you really are, he can keep you from doing what you were created to do, and he can keep you from enjoying the life God has for you.

This is why the devil tirelessly attacks your identity. Every day, his strategy is the same: he accuses, he lies, he condemns. It's all part of his plan to keep you from discovering who you are in Christ and the promises you have been given. The last thing he wants for you to believe is that no matter how many mistakes you have made, it is not too late to begin again!

Whether you've been saved for 30 minutes, 30 days, or 30 years, be aware: you *do* have an enemy. The devil is not just a Halloween character. He is a real adversary, and he wants to keep you from a new beginning. First Peter 5:8 tells us:

> ...Be vigilant and cautious at all times; for that enemy of yours, the devil, roams around like a lion roaring [in fierce hunger], seeking someone to seize upon and devour.

As a young Christian, I went many years without knowing I had an enemy. I never heard a sermon in church about the devil. I didn't know that he wanted to condemn me and keep me tied to defeated attitudes, actions, and mind-sets of the past.

But Jesus made it very clear how the devil operates. In John 10:10 (NIV), Jesus said that the devil "comes only to steal and kill and destroy." The tactics of the enemy shouldn't surprise us. Just like everything else in our lives, the devil wants to steal our identity, kill our sense of worth, and destroy our happiness.

Identity theft isn't a new trick; the enemy has been using this attack for a long time. Consider the young Hebrew men who were taken into Babylonian captivity in Daniel chapter 1. Their names were Hananiah (meaning "Yahweh hath been gracious"), Mishael (meaning "Who is like God?"), and Azariah (meaning "Yahweh has helped"). These men had godly names—godly identities—but those identities were the first things that came under attack.

When captured and exiled to a godless nation, their names were immediately changed. They were no longer identified as Hananiah, Mishael, and Azariah; now they were called Shadrach, Meshach, and Abednego. All three of these new names were related to false, Chaldean gods. The Babylonians knew that if they could cause these Hebrew teenagers to forget who they really were, they could make them prisoners for life.

This attack against identity has significant spiritual applications. It shows us that identity is the very foundation of freedom. When you know who you are in Christ and what has been promised to you in His Word, you refuse to settle for a prisoner mentality.

> *In order to fight for freedom, you must first believe you were born to be free.*

In order to fight for freedom, you must first believe you were born to be free.

Resist The Devil

Though you do have an enemy, I want to be very clear about this today: You have nothing to fear. The devil has no power over you… none! The moment you gave your life to the Lord, you became a redeemed, forgiven, righteous child of God. Satan has no rightful place in your life.

Rather than live in fear of your enemy, you are empowered by God to live a bold, confident, productive, happy life that overcomes the enemy at every turn. You don't ever have to live in worry or doubt, wondering, "Is the enemy going to defeat me today?" The Spirit of God in you is greater than any attack of the devil. The Bible gives you this assurance: "He Who lives in you is greater (mightier) than he who is in the world" (1 John 4:4).

Furthermore, the book of Ephesians says that you are equipped with the "armor of God" so that you can "be strong in the Lord and in his mighty power." It goes on to say that this armor of God will allow you to "take your stand against the devil's schemes." (Ephesians 6:10–11 NIV)

Did you see that? You don't have to run from the devil's schemes; you don't have to just survive the devil's attacks. You are equipped to take a stand. You have the power and authority in Jesus to stand your ground . . . to move forward . . . to begin again.

I want you to really understand what that means. You are no longer a victim of the devil's lies and accusations—you are a warrior, dressed with all the armor you need to defeat the enemy in every area of your life. You have been given . . .

- The belt of truth (living in the truth of Scripture).
- The breastplate of righteousness (knowing you have right standing with God because of Jesus).
- The shoes of peace (walking in the peace of God).
- The shield of faith (believing God's promises).
- The helmet of salvation (hope that is accompanying your salvation).
- The sword of the Spirit (speaking the Word of God).

You have been equipped and empowered to overcome any attack. Now, the Bible says that you must *put on* that armor—this is a conscious decision on your part. The daily decisions you make

> *The daily decisions you make and the words you say are how you actively dress yourself in God's armor.*

and the words you say are how you actively dress yourself in God's armor.

For example, the way you put on the breastplate of righteousness is by receiving the mercy of God and then making the decision to say, "I know who I am. I am the righteousness of God in Christ, and I am going to be bold in the Lord today and act like the person I was created to be." When you do that, you are putting on spiritual armor that covers and protects you. You are claiming your identity.

I suggest you take a few minutes in prayer every morning and say, "Lord, today I put on the armor You have provided for me through Jesus. I thank You that I am righteous today in Christ. I choose to wear the **breastplate of righteousness**. And I thank You that I have the **shield of faith**. Today I will choose to live by faith not by sight, trusting the promises in Your Word. Also, I thank You that You have armed me with the **sword of the Spirit** . . ." And then go through the list of armor found in Ephesians 6:13–17, piece by piece. Confessing these promises out loud helps renew your mind, helps release the blessings of God that are yours, and it reminds the devil that you know your rights as a child of God. Confessing God's Word is one of the ways we release our faith to work on our behalf.

It's amazing to me how many Christians allow the enemy to walk all over them. He has lied to them so many times—saying, "You're not good enough. You messed up too badly. God is angry with you. You don't deserve a second chance," etc.—that they gradually begin to believe his lies and accusations.

You may know exactly what I'm talking about. If you've given up on a dream, stopped praying for a need, turned your back on a promise, or lost a sense of hope, it may be because you're experiencing an identity crisis. Instead of standing on God's Word and knowing who you are in Christ, you have started to identify with your past, your sins, your fears, and your surroundings.

You don't have to live this way. God wants to free you from the bondage of identity crisis and assure you of your identity in Him.

He wants you to live a life full of joy, hope, and purpose. That's His plan for you.

In order to solve an identity crisis, you must understand there is a big difference between your "who" and your "do." In other words, *who* you are is not determined by what you *did* or *do*. Of course you messed up; we all have. Of course you made a mistake; we all have. Of course you want to do better; we all do. But those actions don't identify you—your position in Christ is what identifies you. When the devil tries to tell you otherwise, stand against him.

James 4:7 says it this way: "Resist the devil [stand firm against him], and he will flee from you."

You might say, "Well, Joyce, that sounds easy, but I have no idea how to do that. How do I resist the devil? How do I stand against him? How do I discover my identity?"

Well, I'm glad you asked, because I've got some good news for you…

Your Identity In Christ

The best way to defeat a lie is to know and speak the truth. The next time the enemy lies to you, I want you to use the following list to declare your identity in Christ Jesus.

When the devil asks, "Who do you think you are, believing for healing?" "Who do you think you are, enrolling to go back to school?" "What do you think you're doing? You can't forgive the person who hurt you." "Who do you think you are, trying to make healthy choices?" "You can't change; it is too late," just answer by saying:

- I am the righteousness of God in Jesus Christ. (2 Corinthians 5:21)
- I am forgiven of all my sins. (Ephesians 1:7)
- I am born of God, and the evil one does not touch me. (1 John 5:18)

- I am raised up with Christ and seated in heavenly places. (Ephesians 2:6; Colossians 2:12)
- I am a believer, and the light of the Gospel shines in my mind. (2 Corinthians 4:4)
- I am more than a conqueror through Him Who loves me. (Romans 8:37)
- I am an overcomer by the blood of the Lamb and the word of my testimony. (Revelation 12:11)
- I am the head and not the tail; I am above only and not beneath. (Deuteronomy 28:13)
- I am greatly loved by God. (Romans 1:7; Ephesians 2:4; Colossians 3:12; 1 Thessalonians 1:4)
- I am strengthened with all might according to His glorious power. (Colossians 1:11)
- I am the light of the world. (Matthew 5:14)
- I am a new creature in Christ. (2 Corinthians 5:17)
- I am able to do all things through Christ Jesus. (Philippians 4:13)
- I am redeemed from the curses of sin, sickness, and poverty. (Deuteronomy 28:1–14; Galatians 3:13)
- I am healed by the stripes of Jesus. (Isaiah 53:5; 1 Peter 2:24)
- I am God's workmanship, created in Christ to do good works. (Ephesians 2:10)
- I am a joint-heir with Jesus. (Romans 8:17)

And those are just a few of the *many* things that identify you as a child of the Most High God. I encourage you to do your own study on "identity in Christ," because the list goes on and on.

This is the truth of who you *really* are. You are not identified by your background, your upbringing, your level of education, your mistakes, your highs, or your lows—you are identified by the powerful work of God for you and in you. As a Christian, you have been given the name of Christ Jesus. There is no higher name!

There is a well-known fable told about the legendary conqueror, Alexander the Great...

As a Christian, you have been given the name of Christ Jesus. There is no higher name!

One night while walking through camp, the brilliant commander happened upon a soldier who had fallen asleep while on guard duty. This was a serious offense, one that could be punishable by death.

Sensing movement around him, the soldier woke to find his commander standing above him. He jumped to his feet, fearing for his life. Alexander the Great asked the startled sentry, "Soldier, what is your name?"

"Alexander, sir," the soldier replied with trepidation.

Alexander the Great asked again, "Soldier, what is your name?"

"My name is Alexander, sir."

A third time, Alexander the Great demanded, "Soldier, what is your name?"

And a third time, the soldier answered, "Sir, my name is Alexander."

Alexander the Great looked at the soldier intently and said, "Young man, either change your conduct or change your name."

The young soldier in this story had been given a great name. And he was challenged by his commander to recognize the significance of his name and operate differently than before. It's a powerful picture of identity.

The same is true for us. You and I have been given a great name— the name of Christ. He has become our identity. But unlike the story of Alexander the Great, God isn't angry or disappointed when you fail to live up to His name. The truth is that we all fail from time to time.

You didn't receive Christ through your own efforts or achievements, and you can't maintain your identity in Christ through efforts or achievements. Your identity was a free gift given to you by God because of His great love for you. There will be times when you fall asleep on guard duty—when you mess up and fall short—but His grace is there for you when you do.

This doesn't mean that we take advantage of God's grace. We don't run around purposely doing things that grieve the Holy Spirit. Of course, we desire each day to live in obedience to the Word of God. It just means that we refuse to allow the devil to condemn us when we fall short.

Too Late?

You've been given a powerful new identity in Christ. Don't let the devil tell you that you are anything less than who you are. You are a joint-heir with Christ, loved and approved by God Himself. Spend each day in the confidence of your position in Christ. It is this assurance that will inspire you to make God-honoring choices in your life and to begin pursuing God with a renewed passion.

In my years spent studying and teaching God's Word, I've discovered this important truth: It is never too late to discover your true identity. Whatever you have been through, God wants you to know that you are His son or daughter, and you have more value than you could possibly know.

Today is the day for you to reject the lies of the enemy—don't allow them to hold you back any longer.

> *Maybe a parent said you would never amount to anything.*
> *That was a lie.*
> *It's never too late to discover your true identity.*

Maybe a teacher said you didn't have what it takes to succeed.
That was a lie.
It's never too late to discover your true identity.

Maybe someone abused you, and you feel you're broken and beyond repair.
That is a lie.
It's never too late to discover your true identity.

Maybe a spouse abandoned you, and you believe you're unlovable.
That is a lie.
It's never too late to discover your true identity.

Maybe you failed in a career endeavor, and you feel weak and inadequate.
That is a lie.
It's never too late to discover your true identity.

I believe today is a new beginning for you. It's time to shake off the lies that have held you back for too long. Today is a day of destiny. Today is a day of healing. Today is the day you can say with confidence, "I am a child of God, I am loved, valuable, talented, and forgiven. I know who I am in Christ!"

Summary:

- The enemy will try to attack your identity.
- You have the power and authority in Christ to defeat the devil and reject his lies.
- You have been equipped and empowered with the armor of God.

- There is a big difference between your "who" and your "do." *Who* you are is not defined by what you *did*.
- The identity you have in Christ makes you a brand-new person!
- It's never too late to discover your true identity.

"Moses spent forty years in the king's palace thinking that he was somebody; then he lived forty years in the wilderness finding out that without God he was a nobody; finally he spent forty years discovering how a nobody with God can be a somebody."

—Dwight L. Moody

CHAPTER 8

Finding The YOU In Bea-YOU-tiful

"Do what you can, with what you have, where you are."
—Theodore Roosevelt

When I sat down to write this book, I knew this second section was going to be extremely important. *You Can Begin Again* is a message of hope—it's all about fresh starts and new beginnings. This book is meant to remind you that it is never too late to set out on a new journey with God...in any area of your life. However, no journey is without challenges. I wouldn't be helping you if I didn't tell you about the obstacles along the way.

The Bible uses phrases like *guard your heart* (Proverbs 4:23), *be vigilant and cautious* (1 Peter 5:8), and *be on the watch* (Hebrews 12:15) for a reason. You don't need to fear, but you should be aware: there are saboteurs working to shipwreck your faith before you even leave the harbor. That's why this second section (*What's Stopping You?*) is so crucial.

Through the power of the Holy Spirit, you can overcome any opposition, but in order to do so, you must first know what that opposition is. I don't believe we should ever focus solely on our obstacles—our focus is always on Jesus—but our obstacles are still part of the equation. For example: gaining a victory means *defeating an enemy*; and moving into something new usually means *moving out of something old*. When we make a choice to do the good thing and actually start doing it, we overcome evil with good. However, evil will still try to oppress and tempt us.

Maybe this is why the apostle Paul felt it was important to include this phrase in 2 Corinthians 5:17:

> …The old [previous moral and spiritual condition] has passed away.

Nestled between two phrases that speak of hope for something new, Paul reminds us that letting go of the old is an important part of the process. Here is the whole verse:

> Therefore if any person is [ingrafted] in Christ (the Messiah) he is a new creation (a new creature altogether); the old [previous moral and spiritual condition] has passed away. Behold, the fresh and new has come! (2 Corinthians 5:17)

Old mind-sets, unhealthy relationships, lies of the devil, past hurts, defeated attitudes, crippling habits. These are all obstacles in your discovery that it is never too late to begin again. They are part of the "old" that Paul says has "passed away." The good news is you no longer have to allow these hindrances of the past to affect your present or your future.

Jesus said that we shouldn't sew new patches on old garments and we shouldn't put new wine in old wineskins (Matthew 9:16–17). Many Christians try to keep the old life and just add a few new things to it, but God is offering us something entirely new! We cannot keep mixing the old and the new. Get an entirely new attitude and way of thinking (Ephesians 4:23). That is the road from the old life to the new.

I hope you will keep that in mind as you read this chapter. We began this section by talking about external opposition (the accusations of others and the lies of the enemy), but in this chapter, it's time to get more personal. Over the next few pages, we're going to talk about your own internal opposition. Issues like insecurity, inferiority, regrets, and discouragement are things you can confront and defeat as you move forward with God. With the help of the Holy Spirit you can change these mind-sets, but it will take some brave and bold choices on your part.

> *God's plan for your life is not dependent on your circumstances, your doubts, or even your feelings—His plan is so much bigger than those things.*

I believe God has something important in store for you in this chapter. He is going to help you discover your worth and your destiny in Him. Remember, God's plan for your life is not dependent on your circumstances, your doubts, or even your feelings—His plan is so much bigger than those things.

Lauren Scruggs discovered this to be true. You may remember her story...

Lauren's Story

Model. Fashion journalist. World traveler. It appeared that Lauren Scruggs had it all.

Not only was she beautiful, she was ambitious. Having graduated from college with honors and now completing two internships in New York City, Lauren (called "Lolo" by friends and family) spent her days developing and writing an online fashion journal—it's what she loved to do. Her life was going just the way she planned. Lauren Scruggs seemed to be living the dream. What could possibly go wrong?

The 911 call came in at 8:48 p.m. on December 3, 2011:

Dispatcher: "911. What is your emergency?"
Caller: "A girl walked into an airplane [propeller]. I need an ambulance immediately!"

Dispatcher: "Was it moving when it happened?"

Caller: "Yes...she's on the ground...she's not moving."

That was the night Lauren Scruggs's life changed, and that was the night she was thrust onto the world stage.

Lauren's story has been told by news agencies all over the globe. After attending church with her family that December night, Lauren went for a flight with friends in a small, single-engine prop plane above Dallas, Texas, to see the Christmas lights.

The flight was smooth and uneventful, but moments after landing, a freak accident on the tarmac threatened to take Lauren's life. Upon exiting the airplane, the young model mistakenly turned the wrong way and walked into the plane's still-spinning propeller. When the paramedics arrived at the scene of the accident, they wondered if she would even survive the night.

Lauren was rushed to a hospital where medical personnel worked feverishly to save her life. With her family and friends praying through the night and a team of tireless surgeons working heroically, fear turned to relief with the announcement that Lauren would survive. But now new issues arose: No one was sure how her body would respond to the extensive injuries.

The propeller struck Lauren's head and the left side of her body. Her injuries included a skull fracture, a broken collarbone, the loss of her left eye, and the loss of her left hand. It was a miracle that she survived the accident, but doctors cautioned it might take many more miracles for a full recovery. "Would she wake up with the same personality?" "Would she ever be able to form a sentence again?" These were questions no one had answers for. Lauren's parents, Jeff and Cheryl Scruggs, were told to brace for the worst.

In an interview for *I Am Second*, Cheryl recalls that night:

> *The very first night [Lauren] had surgery for about eight hours...I felt helpless. As a mom, you never dream that your*

*child is going to go through anything like this... There was
nothing I could do to change it. But I did know that [Lauren]
had a deep faith and that was what was so amazing. I knew
that as we made the steps for the future and into the future,
that God would be our rock. Jesus would be our stronghold,
and that's what we had to rely on.*

As news of Lauren's accident attracted national and international
attention, people all around the world began praying and sending
thoughts of encouragement to the Scruggs family. Millions followed
her recovery and celebrated the news that Lauren suffered no brain
damage or impairment of her personality.

In the time since the accident, Lauren has gone through significant physical rehabilitation, and the emotional adjustments to the
loss of her eye and her hand haven't been easy. But through it all,
her courage and strength have been nothing short of amazing. The
world got to witness a young woman who trusts God and finds
strength through her faith in Him.

In her first television interview after the accident, Lauren said:

*Emotionally, days are hard sometimes, just accepting the loss
of my eye and my hand, but it just gets better. I realize God
is in control of my life, and there is a purpose in this story.
Spiritually, I've just learned to live by faith and not by sight.
Even though I've lost my left eye, I just realize the Lord has a
strong purpose in it, and I need to use that.*

In another interview, she said:

*I think I'm seeing that this life is way bigger than me, and I
think a lot of things I held important earlier in my career were
quite shallow. I just want to use what I've been through to talk
to young girls and let them know our appearance is not what*

defines us. Insecurities that we hold on to don't define us. The Lord is just a sweet place to go.

Lauren "Lolo" Scruggs is an inspiration to us all. She refuses to let difficult circumstances ruin her life. She could have felt sorry for herself and given up on her future, but instead, she found a new purpose—a new beginning—and she is living life to the fullest. On November 16, 2012, Lauren told NBC's *The Today Show*: "I've learned to appreciate life a lot more. My joy in life has intensified, and even my compassion for people has strengthened."

Appreciate life? Intensified joy? Stronger compassion? Maybe Lauren Scruggs is living the dream after all.

Refusing To Be Controlled By Your Feelings

If someone was looking for reasons to get discouraged and give up, Lauren Scruggs had plenty. She could have easily settled into a victim mentality—no one would blame her. I'm sure there were many times that fear, insecurity, doubt, and a host of other feelings tried to sink her faith. But Lauren refused to live her life subject to those feelings. Instead, she has chosen to make the most of each day and trust that God has a wonderful plan for her life. We should all live that way. Please notice that I said she *chose*. Are you willing to make a healthy choice regarding your own insecurities?

What imagined deficiency or handicap in your life is holding you back? Remember, you are much more than the way you look, or what your job title is in the workplace, and there is no one else on Earth exactly like you. Since you are one of a kind, that makes you rare and extremely valuable. Learn to be secure in God's love for you. Be yourself and stand against insecurity like you would a thief trying to break into your home.

> *Since you are one of a kind, that makes you rare and extremely valuable.*

I think one of the reasons many people are so unhappy in life is that they live as captives to their own feelings. You may be surprised to know that it's not always the influence of others or the attack of the devil that keeps many people from a new level of joy and victory in their lives—it's their own internal issues. Their happiness (or lack of happiness) is dependent on how they feel at any particular moment. If things are going well and they feel good about the events of the day, they think: "Hallelujah! Life is super! Praise God for today!" But the minute something happens to change their mood, watch out! Things can go downhill quickly:

"Hallelujah!" turns to *"How could this happen?"*
"Life is super!" turns to *"Life stinks!"*
"Praise God for today!" turns to *"Blame God for today!"*

Their security, peace, and joy are connected to their circumstances. If things are going well, they feel loved, but if they are not going well, then they think God doesn't love them or that they are being punished for some sin they committed.

I used to live this way. For years, I went through life captive to my feelings. I might be having a great day, but the moment someone said something that upset me, made me feel insecure, or the moment something happened that worried me, my day was immediately ruined. And whatever I was feeling on any given day determined my behavior and affected my relationship with God.

Thankfully, the Lord delivered me from the cruel taskmaster of fickle feelings. The more I studied His Word, the more I began to see that I was called to be led by the Word and the Spirit, not led by my soul (mind, will, and emotions). I learned that I might not be able to control what thought popped into my mind or what feeling arose in my heart, but I could control what I *did* with that thought or feeling. I no longer had to let negative, destructive feelings rule my life; instead, I could take authority over my own emotions, submit them to God, and choose to stand on the Word of God. This was a powerful revelation that, in many ways, gave me a fresh start in my life. (If this is an issue in your life, I suggest you read my book on the subject, *Living Beyond Your Feelings*.)

A lot of Christians are blaming the devil for their own self-inflicted wounds. But when you're beating yourself up and putting yourself down, the devil can move on to someone else; you've already come under attack...from yourself.

Let me show you what I'm talking about. Here are three feelings that keep a lot of believers from living the abundant, joy-filled life Jesus came to give them. (Warning: These may hit close to home.)

1. Insecurity

Insecurity is at epic proportions in our society. It seems we come across touchy, insecure people everywhere we go...including the Church. Insecurity keeps people so focused on their perceived weaknesses they can't see anything else. They live in fear and with a "failure mentality" because insecurity is influencing every decision they make. Their thoughts are focused on what people think of them, rather than how they can be a blessing to others.

Insecurities are often born from hurtful things others have said about you or lies the enemy tells you, but they grow only when you decide to nurture them.

As a child of God, you don't have to live under the storm clouds of insecurity. When you choose to receive your acceptance and self-worth from God, you will never need to be insecure around people again. God wants you to live with a bold confidence, believing in faith that His plans and purposes will come to pass in your life. Good

> *When you choose to receive your acceptance and self-worth from God, you will never need to be insecure around people again.*

things don't happen in our lives because of us; often they happen in spite of us. They are the result of God's love, mercy, and grace. Believe by faith that all things are possible with God—including Him doing great things for and through you!

- Insecurity whispers, "You can't do this because you're too weak, inexperienced, hurt, or broken."
  Faith shouts: "I have strength for all things in Christ Who empowers me!" (Philippians 4:13)
- Insecurity whispers, "Why try? That's impossible for you to do."
  Faith shouts: "All things are possible with God!" (Matthew 19:26)
- Insecurity whispers, "You're not talented enough, attractive enough, or smart enough."
  Faith shouts: "I am fearfully and wonderfully made!" (Psalm 139:14 NIV)

I'm not talking about some sort of trivial self-help technique. I'm encouraging you to believe and speak God's Word in order to defeat a dangerous enemy—an enemy that comes only to kill, steal, and destroy.

In Numbers chapter 13, the Hebrew spies gave a very troubling report to Moses and the people. They spent 40 days exploring the Promised Land, but when they returned from their mission it was obvious their confidence was shaken. You can practically hear the insecurity in their voices as they said, "...We were in our own sight as grasshoppers, and so we were in their sight" (Numbers 13:33). They didn't just say, "Our enemies think we are small, insignificant bugs." They said, "*We* think we are small, insignificant bugs!" Sadly, this insecurity kept these men and everyone who listened to them from entering the Promised Land.

You don't have to let the same thing happen to you today. God has arranged for you to have a life filled with wonderful things. He doesn't want you to spend your years wandering in the wilderness; He wants you to receive everything that Jesus died to give you. Yes, there will be battles along the way, and there will be times when you feel inadequate for the task. It's in these moments that you reject those old feelings of insecurity and trust in the Lord to fight your battles for you. Don't shrink back...charge forward! Always remember that your faith in God will ultimately win every battle.

Hebrews 10:39 (NIV) says it this way: "But we do not belong to those who shrink back and are destroyed, but to those who have faith and are saved."

2. Regrets And Dreads

Another source of internal opposition is the dangerous duo of regrets and dreads. These two go hand-in-hand and are equally rooted in fear. Regrets cause you to fear the consequences of past mistakes, and dreads cause you to fear the consequences of future mishaps. Both assume the worst; neither are from God.

I remember correcting my son, David, when he was a teenager. He did something he shouldn't have, and I was explaining to him why it was a wrong decision and how I expected him to act differently in the future. What he said to me in response to my correction sent me into a tailspin of regret. He said, "Well, I wouldn't be the way I am if you wouldn't have treated me the way you did." David was old enough by then to know that I had been abused and that I often admitted I was overcoming behavior problems that developed from my dysfunctional past. He was also sly enough to try to use it as a cover-up for his own bad behavior.

I felt really terrible for the rest of the day. When David was younger and I was working through some of my own problems, I probably did a little more yelling at him than my other children. All I could think about were the parenting mistakes I must have made. "I should have done this better." "I could have done that better." "It's all my fault. He's going to be scarred for life." (If you're a parent, you probably know what I'm talking about. There is no *How To Be A Perfect Parent* manual available in bookstores.) There is no child who ever had parents that never made a mistake in their parenting journey.

Can you see how those thoughts I was rehearsing were fear-based? I was regretting my shortcomings and dreading their consequences, afraid that I had ruined my son for life. But in the middle of my regret-and-dread pity party, the Holy Spirit spoke to me. He said, *Joyce, David has the same opportunity to overcome as you did. Not everybody has to be treated perfectly in life to have good character.* God offers us victory in the midst of difficulty, not in the absence of it.

> God offers us victory in the midst of difficulty, not in the absence of it.

What a freeing revelation that was. Immediately, I went from a fear-based mind-set to a faith-based mind-set. Instead of believing, "I messed everything up—things are going to be terrible," I chose to believe God and trust: "God can redeem my shortcomings—I'm believing Him for good things." I went right back to David's room and shared with him what God had spoken to me. It turned out to be a great lesson for both of us.

The same principle is true in any area of your life where regrets and dreads are not confronted. These are unhealthy, fear-based cares that will drag you down and keep you from new levels of victory in your life. If you're afraid of your past and afraid of your future, you'll be frozen in a dysfunctional present. There is only one solution, and it comes straight from 1 Peter 5:7—"Casting the whole of your care [all your anxieties, all your worries, all your concerns, once and for all] on Him, for He cares for you affectionately and cares about you watchfully." Cast those cares off of your life and never pick them up again. God is a God of justice, and that means that He makes every wrong thing right if we trust Him to do so.

Now, if you can make restitution for something you did in the past and make it better, by all means you should do that. However, if there is nothing you can do about a mistake or shortcoming from your past, the best thing you can do is let it go. It's not going to do you any good to bury yourself in regret. Regret is not faith. Regret is basically saying God can't take care of that issue. It is declaring that our mistakes are greater than God's mercy, and that is simply not true. Our "badness" is not greater than God's "goodness."

Hebrews 8:12 says: "For I will be merciful and gracious toward their sins and I will remember their deeds of unrighteousness no more." If God chooses to forgive and forget your sins, you should choose to forgive yourself and forget your sins, too.

3. Discouragement

Missionary William Ward said discouragement is "dissatisfaction with the past, distaste for the present, and distrust of the future." If you've dealt with discouragement in your life, you know that is true. Discouragement steals the zeal that we need for living. It makes us believe that we will fail before we have even tried to succeed.

The experiences from my own life and ministry to others have shown me that discouragement is a feeling we have to deal with on a pretty regular basis. It tries to creep into our lives with even the smallest things. You oversleep and miss your morning workout... discouraged. You fail to get everything crossed off your to-do list for the day... discouraged. You work hard to impress your spouse, but it goes unnoticed... discouraged.

There is nothing wrong with feeling disappointed about something, dealing with it, and moving on—that's a natural reaction when something doesn't go as you hoped it would. But discouragement doesn't let you move on. Discouragement stays with you, stealing your joy, your energy, and clouding your judgment.

In the Word of God, we see that David dealt with discouragement.

In 1 Samuel chapter 30, David and his men returned from a battle only to discover the enemy had plundered their homes. David's men were angry, and he was discouraged. Verse 4 says David "wept until [he] had no more strength to weep." Have you ever been there? Have you ever been so discouraged that the only thing you could do was cry until there were no more tears? Well, if you have, you have a friend in David. He knew what it was like to feel the weight of discouragement.

But the Bible tells us that David didn't let that feeling control his life. He stood up to discouragement, refusing to be captive to it. Look at what the Word says David did to battle discouragement: "David encouraged and strengthened himself in the Lord his God" (1 Samuel 30:6). Another verse tells us that David spoke to his soul when he felt downcast, saying, "Why are you cast down, O my inner self?...Hope in God and wait expectantly for Him" (Psalm 43:5).

David didn't accept discouragement, he didn't give in to it, and he didn't merely put up with it...he aggressively came against it. When he began to feel those unhealthy, ungodly thoughts and feelings, David spoke to his spirit, encouraging himself in the Lord—and we can do the same thing.

> David didn't accept discouragement, he didn't give in to it, and he didn't merely put up with it...he aggressively came against it.

You don't have to live captive to the feelings of discouragement any longer. The moment you begin to feel despair or discouragement—whether it be over something big or something small—remind yourself of God's goodness in your life. Tell yourself, "No, I am not going to live in discouragement. God has been too good to me for me to do that. Why are you cast down, O my inner self? I am going to hope in God and wait expectantly for Him in this situation!"

Don't let insecurity, regrets and dreads, or discouragement ruin your life. Others may live captive to unhealthy and ungodly feelings, but you don't have to. As a child of God, you can make the daily choice to live by the Spirit instead of living by your emotions. And when you do, something amazing happens...

> *If we live by the [Holy] Spirit, let us also walk by the Spirit. [If by the Holy Spirit we have our life in God, let us **go forward** walking in line, our conduct controlled by the Spirit.]* (Galatians 5:25, emphasis added)

With God, you always go forward... never backward. Forward into something new. Forward into something better. Forward into destiny.

Summary:

- Internal opposition is as dangerous as external opposition. You don't have to live captive to unhealthy, ungodly feelings.
- Regardless of your circumstances, you can live a joyful, overcoming life.
- When you receive your acceptance and self-worth in God, insecurity becomes a thing of the past.
- God has forgiven you of your sins. Now it's time to forgive yourself.
- The best way to battle discouragement is to speak to your spirit like David did—encourage yourself in the Lord!

How to...

E ncourage yourself with the promises from God's Word (1 Samuel 30:6).

N o condemnation is from the Lord. Live in the power of grace (Romans 8:1).

J oy is for the journey. Choose to be joyful regardless of your circumstances (Romans 15:13).

O bey when the Lord speaks to you (Deuteronomy 11:26–27).

Y esterday is over. Refuse to live in the past (Philippians 3:13–14).

Y ou can choose to think positive thoughts and to have a good attitude (Philippians 4:8).

O utlaw "stinking thinking." Take every ungodly thought captive (2 Corinthians 10:5).

U se your gifts and talents to help others (Romans 12:13).

R emember what God has done for you. Be thankful (Psalm 103:2).

L ive by faith, not feelings (2 Corinthians 5:7).

I nvite Christ into every area of your life (1 Corinthians 6:19–20).

F orgive those who hurt you (Ephesians 4:32).

E xpect God's goodness in every situation (Psalm 27:14).

CHAPTER 9

Defeating Unexpected Giants

"A ship is safe in harbor, but that's not what ships are for."
—William G. T. Shedd

Goliath was a giant, an unwelcome obstacle. No doubt the armies of Israel had heard of him, and they heard exaggerated tales of his many victories in battle—his size and skill were probably legendary. You have to remember, Goliath stood over nine feet tall. The Bible calls him the Philistine "champion" (1 Samuel 17:4). Undefeated... arrogant...the best of the best. The soldiers in Israel's army knew all about Goliath. And they were afraid.

But David wasn't a soldier (not yet), and he wasn't fighting on the battle lines. David was a shepherd boy, running errands for his dad. His task was to bring food to three of his older brothers, Eliab, Abinadab, and Shammah, who were frontline soldiers in the battle against the Philistines. If David had a to-do list for the day, it probably looked something like this: *(1) Take food to brothers. (2) Come home. (3) Watch the sheep.*

So you see, Goliath was an unexpected obstacle. David didn't wake up that morning planning to go one-on-one with a giant. Perhaps he hadn't practiced his slingshot toss in a few days. He hadn't spent the morning drawing up battle plans or writing victory speeches. If anything, danger and difficulty were probably the last things on David's mind. After all, the prophet Samuel had just anointed him to be king one chapter earlier—promises were made, blessings were given. It was obvious that God had a great plan for David's life. That meant life should go smoothly, right?

But that day it looked like those promises were in danger. The appearance of a "giant" problem had the potential to undo all that was done. David was going about his day, trying to do what was right, and an obstacle showed up in his path. *Trouble. Pressure. Goliath.*

In many ways, you can probably relate to David. Some of the most difficult challenges you've faced in life may be the ones you never saw coming. Minor or major, physical or emotional, inconvenient or devastating—the unexpected pressures can be the most frustrating. Your car breaks down, a trusted friend betrays you, you get laid off from your job, your child rebels, the bill is larger than you thought, a negative diagnosis is given. These disappointments (and others like them) are the "giants" in life that can be the hardest to overcome simply because you weren't expecting them and don't feel ready to overcome them. You were going about your day, trying to do what was right, and an obstacle showed up in your path. *Trouble. Pressure. Goliath.*

New Strength

I know exactly how that feels. I've experienced unforeseen troubles too. I know how frustrating and discouraging these "giants" can be. That's why I wanted to write about them in this chapter. Over the previous chapters, we've seen how the accusation of others, the lies of the devil, and even our own unhealthy feelings try to keep us from the best life God has for us, but sometimes the most difficult obstacles we face are just the pressures of life—unforeseen trials that surprise us, sap our strength, and steal our joy.

Have you ever noticed that these "giants" seem to show up the very minute you're close to victory in a particular area?

- You've been working for months to get out of debt. You're just one month away from financial freedom...an unexpected bill arrives.
- You decide to get in shape, so you begin a new exercise routine. Just when you start to see some progress...you suffer an injury.
- You've been praying that your child will follow God, and just when you think he is back on the right path...he makes a bad decision and gets into trouble.
- You've been praying that the Lord will help you forgive someone who hurt you. You're finally ready to make the choice to forgive...he does something to hurt you again.

Not only do difficult circumstances hit us when we're not expecting them, they can hit us when we're at our most vulnerable. You were *so* close, you were *so* hopeful, you were *so* excited...you finally began to relax and think, "My troubles are over," but now it's back to square one.

I think this is what causes many people to give up. They decide it's too much to overcome, so they throw their hands up in the air and declare, "I've had it! It's just too hard!" Sadly, though they were once so close to victory, they live in defeat: they stay in debt, they never get in shape, they stop praying, they hold on to bitterness. They give in to the pressure. Goliath wins.

But that's not God's plan for His people. Let me make that more personal: That's not God's plan for YOU! You don't have to be overcome and overwhelmed by the pressures of life. No matter how big your problem appears, you can defeat it with God's help and enjoy victory.

> *You don't have to be overcome and overwhelmed by the pressures of life. No matter how big your problem appears, you can defeat it with God's help and enjoy victory.*

You might think, *"I'm just tired. It seems like I don't have the strength for another battle."* Well, can I be honest with you? I'm glad you realize you don't have strength for the battle—because if you try to fight in your own strength, you'll lose every time. The only way you are going to really, truly live in victory is by trusting God in your weaknesses, depending completely on Him for strength. When we bring our problem to God—asking Him to help us overcome it instead of trusting in our own efforts—the Bible says that He will give us all the strength we need.

> *But those who wait for the Lord [who expect, look for, and hope in Him] shall change and renew their strength and power; they shall lift their wings and mount up [close to God] as eagles [mount up to the sun]; they shall run and not be weary, they shall walk and not faint or become tired.* (Isaiah 40:31)

If you'll receive it, that verse can change your entire outlook when dealing with the pressures you face on a daily basis. You aren't called just to get by, just hang in there, or just survive another day—the Bible says God will fill you with strength and power. You're called to "run and not be weary...walk and not faint or become tired."

Depressed, exhausted, joyless Christians have not yet discovered the truth of that promise—or they've forgotten it. They are living as victims of the world's pressures. If that is you, today can be the day you turn things around and experience the abundant, powerful, overcoming life Jesus came to give you. Today can be the day to begin again!

Faith completely turns the tables on your problems. Instead of thinking your problem is too great, you realize that "greater is He who is in me" (1 John 4:4 NASB). Instead of being discouraged by difficulties, you begin to laugh at your problems (Nehemiah 8:10).

Instead of feeling anxiety over your situation, you have a bold confidence that God is going to do something amazing (Proverbs 3:26).

I like to say it this way: "God gives you the strength to press against the pressure that's pressing you!" This is a new mind-set that I encourage you to embrace. Don't be afraid of your problem, don't be stressed out by your problem, and don't be discouraged by your problem—attack the problem that is attacking you. This is a biblical, faith-filled attitude that can

> *"God gives you the strength to press against the pressure that's pressing you!"*

revolutionize your life. It certainly did for David. His response to Goliath in 1 Samuel 17 changed everything. The shepherd boy was beginning to look like a king...

The Unexpected Enemy Gets An Unexpected Response

When the Philistine came forward to meet David, David ran quickly toward the battle line to meet the Philistine. (I Samuel 17:48)

Keep in mind, the typical response when Goliath walked onto the battlefield was fear and trembling. The very sight of this larger-than-life enemy intimidated his opponents. And if his size wasn't enough to scare you, his booming threats certainly were—his opponents would run in fear when Goliath started predicting doom to anyone who dared to stand against him.

This is exactly what was happening in 1 Samuel 17 when David arrived on the scene. Goliath was up to his usual tricks of intimidation—defying, threatening, and cursing the armies of Israel—the soldiers were shrinking back in fear. Verse 24 tells us,

"All the men of Israel, when they saw the man, fled from him, terrified." No one is willing to attack this enemy—not one person.

But when David showed up on the battle lines to deliver food to his brothers, the story began to change. David didn't get upset that he had an unexpected problem; he decided to deal with it. And because he realized that his strength came from God, David wasn't intimidated by Goliath the way everyone else seemed to be. In verse 26, David asked an amazing question: "What shall be done for the man who kills this Philistine and takes away the reproach from Israel?"

David didn't ask, "Why is this happening to me?" or question God by asking, "Lord, how could You allow this to take place?" Those are questions born out of worry and anxiety. Those are questions that assume your problem is greater than your Provider. David knew that God is greater than any obstacle he could ever face, so he basically asked, "What happens when I win?" Where everyone else saw an obstacle, David saw an opportunity. David lived out in the fields tending sheep. It gave him lots of time to be alone, get to know God intimately, worship Him, and become strong through that relationship. David was prepared to face whatever came his way.

> *Where everyone else saw an obstacle, David saw an opportunity.*

Read what David said to this unexpected giant:

> *Then said David to the Philistine, You come at me with a sword, a spear, and a javelin, but I come to you in the name of the Lord of hosts, the God of the ranks of Israel, Whom you have defied.*
>
> *This day the Lord will deliver you into my hand, and I will smite you and cut off your head. And I will give the corpses of the army of the Philistines this day to the birds of the air and the wild beasts of the earth, that all the earth may know that there is a God in Israel.*

> *And all this assembly shall know that the Lord saves not with sword and spear; for the battle is the Lord's, and He will give you into our hands. (1 Samuel 17:45–47)*

David speaks to his problem, and he focuses on God. (In those verses, David mentions the Lord seven times.) He knows the victory isn't dependent on his own best efforts—God is the One who will win the victory. Filled with confidence, David responds in a way that Goliath wasn't ready for—he attacks the giant. David presses against the pressure that was pressing him.

> *...David ran quickly toward the battle line to meet the Philistine. (1 Samuel 17:48)*

If you're familiar with the Bible, you know that David won a great victory that day. Armed with nothing more than a slingshot and faith in God, David defeated Goliath, and the armies of Israel routed the Philistines. It is an amazing testimony of what can happen when you boldly confront the obstacles in your life. When you press against the pressure that's pressing you, God is glorified and giants fall.

My Goliath Today Weighs Seven Pounds

Not every giant is huge. Sometimes small giants can be very aggravating. I have a seven-pound Maltese dog. Her name is Duchess, just in case you want to pray for her potty problem! She is, of course, house-trained and has been for a number of years. But one week, she had an accident in the basement. Shortly after that, Dave took her for a long walk, and when she walked inside the house, she had another accident on our floor! What! She NEVER does that! After we corrected her and she did her "pitiful act," trying to get out of trouble, we looked for the pet spray that takes away dog potty odors and of course we couldn't find it anywhere...probably because she never acts this way. I mean REALLY...I wanted to write about giants, not have one! The obstacles we face do not have to be "big" to be considered something giant; all it has to do is cause distress in your life—it has to be an unexpected enemy or obstacle.

Taking A New Approach

I want you to think for a minute about that unexpected enemy you may be facing today. I don't know exactly what you're going through—it's different for all of us—maybe you're facing a financial issue, a health issue, a relational issue, a work issue, or some major disappointment. You thought the battle would be over by now, or maybe you never thought you'd have to fight this battle in the first place, but here it is, standing in front of you. It could be that, like Goliath, your problem seems impossibly big and threatens to be more than you can handle. If it's stealing your peace and keeping you from enjoying the life God has for you, it's time to deal with it.

I know it seems that problems often appear when we least expect them, but the truth is we shouldn't be surprised when we face trouble, big or small. Jesus warned us that these things would come. He said in John 16:33:

> *"I have told you these things, so that in Me you may have [perfect] peace and confidence. In the world you have tribulation and trials and distress and frustration; but be of good cheer [take courage; be confident, certain, undaunted]! For I have overcome the world. [I have deprived it of power to harm you and have conquered it for you.]"*

Because the world we live in is broken and full of sin, we will face problems on this side of eternity. But don't be discouraged; Jesus gave us a great promise. He said that even when we face troubles in life we can "be of good cheer [take courage; be confident, certain, undaunted]!" for He has overcome the world. You don't have to focus on your problem. Focus on Jesus—He has overcome your problem! The battle has already been won and all we need to do is take steps of faith and obedience, realizing that each step is leading us closer and closer to experiencing the victory that is already ours in Christ.

Whatever "giant" you are up against, I want you to take a new approach: Instead of comparing that obstacle to *your* ability, compare that obstacle to *God's* ability. You see, the soldiers hiding from Goliath were all making the wrong comparison. They were looking at Goliath…then looking at themselves. They knew that Goliath was bigger than they were, so they hid in fear. *How could they possibly win?* But David made a different comparison. David looked at Goliath… then he looked at God. He knew that Goliath was smaller than God, so he ran in faith, instead of in fear. *How could he possibly lose?*

Your problem may be bigger than you are today, but it's not bigger than God. If you had to face it on your own, you'd be in trouble, but you don't have to face it on your own.

> Your problem may be bigger than you are today, but it's not bigger than God.

God is for you, and He can overcome any enemy or obstacle that threatens to hurt you. I realize you didn't see it coming, but God did. He is not surprised or intimidated by oversized obstacles—He defeated giants before, and He can do it again. Defeating giants is God's specialty. What looks like an obstacle is actually an opportunity. Don't be afraid of the pressure. Press back and watch the giants fall.

Summary:

- You are called to soar above the pressures of life (Isaiah 40:31).
- The key to winning the battle over your giant is trusting God for the strength you need.

- Instead of asking, "Why is this happening to me?" start asking, "What happens when I win?"
- Press against the pressure that's pressing you.
- Your problem may be bigger than you are, but it's never bigger than God.

A Formula for Defeating Giants

1. David ignored the criticism and unbelief of others.

> David said to Saul, Let no man's heart fail because of this Phi-
> listine; your servant will go out and fight with him. And Saul
> said to David, You are not able to go to fight against this Phi-
> listine. You are only an adolescent, and he has been a warrior
> from his youth. (1 Samuel 17:32–33)

YOU CAN ignore the criticism and unbelief of others.

> For it is God's will and intention that by doing right [your
> good and honest lives] should silence (muzzle, gag) the igno-
> rant charges and ill-informed criticisms of foolish persons.
> (1 Peter 2:15)

> … If God is for us, who [can be] against us? [Who can be our
> foe, if God is on our side?] (Romans 8:31)

2. David remembered the victories God gave him in the past.

> Your servant killed both the lion and the bear; and this uncir-
> cumcised Philistine shall be like one of them, for he has defied
> the armies of the living God! David said, The Lord Who deliv-
> ered me out of the paw of the lion and out of the paw of the
> bear, He will deliver me out of the hand of this Philistine.
> (1 Samuel 17:36–37)

YOU CAN remember the victories God gave you in the past.

> Only take heed, and guard your life diligently, lest you forget
> the things which your eyes have seen and lest they depart from
> your [mind and] heart all the days of your life. (Deuteronomy
> 4:9)

And they overcome (conquered) him by means of the blood of the Lamb and by the utterance of their testimony... (Revelation 12:11)

3. David spoke positive words of victory, not defeat.

This day the Lord will deliver you into my hand...the battle is the Lord's, and He will give you into our hands. (1 Samuel 17:46–47)

YOU CAN speak positive words of victory, not defeat.

Let the redeemed of the Lord say so... (Psalm 107:2)

Yet amid all these things we are more than conquerors and gain a surpassing victory through Him Who loved us. (Romans 8:37)

4. David used the unique gifts and abilities God had given him. He didn't try to be somebody else.

Saul clothed David with his armor...And David said to Saul, I cannot go with these, for I am not used to them. And David took them off. Then he took his staff in his hand and chose five smooth stones out of the brook and put them in his shepherd's [lunch] bag...and his sling was in his hand. (1 Samuel 17:38–40)

YOU CAN use the unique gifts and abilities God has given you. Don't try to be somebody else.

For we are God's [own] handiwork (His workmanship)... (Ephesians 2:10)

I praise you because I am fearfully and wonderfully made... (Psalm 139:14 NIV)

5. David was totally dependent on God and he gave God all the glory.

> Then said David to the Philistine, You come to me with a sword, a spear, and a javelin, but I come to you in the name of the Lord of hosts, the God of the ranks of Israel, Whom you have defied. This day the Lord will deliver you into my hand…all the earth may know that there is a God in Israel. (1 Samuel 17:45–46)

YOU CAN be totally dependent on God and give God all the glory.

> Lean on, trust in, and be confident in the Lord with all your heart and mind and do not rely on your own insight or understanding. (Proverbs 3:5)

> Call on Me in the day of trouble; I will deliver you, and you shall honor and glorify Me. (Psalm 50:15)

6. David attacked his problem; he ran to his enemy.

> When the Philistine came forward to meet David, David ran quickly toward the battle line to meet the Philistine. David put his hand into his bag and took out a stone and slung it… (1 Samuel 17:48–49)

YOU CAN attack your problem; run to your enemy.

> For by You I can run through a troop, and by my God I can leap over a wall. (Psalm 18:29)

> Be strong, courageous, and firm; fear not nor be in terror before them, for it is the Lord your God Who goes with you; He will not fail you or forsake you. (Deuteronomy 31:6)

CHAPTER 10

On Your Mark...Get Set...GO!

"The way to get started is quit talking and begin doing."
—Walt Disney

Imagine with me that it's a brisk spring day. The last snow has melted, the flowers are budding, and your neighbor woke you up mowing his lawn a week earlier than was necessary. With the warmer weather, your local Starbucks is advertising new iced coffee flavors, and every clothing store in town is already selling bathing suits. Spring is here.

You breathe in the early morning air as you sit gathered with hundreds of other families, excited to cheer your son on in his first race of the year. Actually, his first race ever. He usually plays baseball in the spring, but he surprised you this year when he told you he wanted to go out for Track and Field. And he surprised you even more when he came bounding into the house two weeks earlier and excitedly announced, "I MADE THE TEAM!" You knew he was fast, but you had no idea he was *that* fast! You smiled as you thought to yourself, "He obviously gets his athleticism from me."

Moments earlier, before arriving at the neighborhood middle school, you gave him the same speech you've been giving since he was five years old. Whether it was soccer, baseball, music, or academics, you say the same thing each time: "Remember, I'm proud of you no matter what happens. I just want you to go out there and do your very best. I'll be cheering for you as loud as I can." He nodded his head knowingly. The only thing he said before getting out of the car was, "Man, I'm really nervous."

The bleacher seats are terribly uncomfortable, and as the runners arrive at their assigned lanes, you make a mental note to bring a lawn chair or a cushion for the next meet. Now the race is about to begin. You cheer wildly as your son's name is announced over the loudspeaker, and you say a silent prayer as he settles into the starting blocks.

The enthusiastic crowd quiets as the starter announces: "Runners, take your mark...get set...GO!" And that's when it happens—he freezes. The other runners shoot out of the blocks and down the track, but not your son. He sits crouched at the starting line; he hasn't taken a step. The announcer snaps again, "Go!" *He doesn't move.* You yell as loudly as you can, "GO...GO...GO!!!" *Nothing.* For some reason, he sits in the starting blocks. He hasn't joined the race. He's stuck at "get set."

As a parent, how would you feel if the above scenario were a true one? What if you knew your child was ready for the race, but you could see that he was letting his own nervousness or insecurities keep him from taking a single step? You wouldn't be angry or upset, but you'd likely be frustrated, and more than anything you would be disappointed for him. I bet you'd have an important conversation with him on the way home. If you are like me, it would sound something like this: "Son, you can't win a race if you stay in the starting blocks. I have confidence in you, but you have to have confidence in yourself. Don't let nerves or anxiety keep you from doing what you love. Go out there and do your best. Good things will happen...but you've got to take that first step!"

> *"Go out there and do your best. Good things will happen...but you've got to take that first step!"*

Stuck At "Get Set…"

I tell you that story because I've noticed there are a lot of Christians stuck in the starting blocks. They aren't sure how a situation is going to turn out, or exactly what they should do, so they do nothing. Instead of running the race that God has set out for them (see Hebrews 12:1), they are letting worry and anxiety keep them frozen at the starting line.

In different areas of our lives, God has been reminding us through the pages of this book that, with Him, it's never too late. It's never too late to overcome fear, restore a relationship, start a career, go back to school, preach the Gospel, improve your health—the list goes on and on. But here is a truth that applies to each and every situation: It's never too late… *if* you are willing to take a step.

God wants you to participate in the miracle He is doing in your life. If you think that you're going to wake up one day and supernaturally be at the finish line, you're going to be disappointed. It doesn't work that way. In our relationship with God, each one of us is given the great opportunity to walk out our faith. Just as Adam and Eve walked with God in the cool of the garden, just as the disciples walked with Jesus on the roads of Galilee, we are called to walk with the Lord on a daily basis. But in order to walk, you have to do something—you have to take the steps that God leads you to take. Just as the runner who was stuck at "get set" was being encouraged by the coach, the crowd, and his parents to "GO," God is encouraging us to step out and be all we can be.

But many times, because we aren't sure of *all* the steps, we don't even take the first one. We're waiting for God to tell us how the next five years of our lives are going to work out, and God is telling us what to do today. I've learned in my relationship with God that He doesn't always give me the entire plan; He usually just gives me the *next* step. God keeps secrets and hides things from us so we will walk in faith and continue seeking Him. He always reveals what we need to know at the right time.

You may want to have a ministry that reaches the world, but God is asking you to take *step one*—share the Gospel with your neighbor across the street. You may be praying that God will give you your own business, but God is asking you to take *step one*—show up for work on time and be faithful at the job you have now. You may be trying to figure out how to lose a certain amount of weight, but God wants you to take *step one*—exercise for 20 minutes today. We have a tendency to get so wrapped up in the destination that we never even begin the journey. What is God asking you to do today?

Faith is always active—always. It is not a passive endeavor. Faith requires that you move forward into what God is telling you to do. Sometimes people say to me, "Joyce, because

> *Faith is always active—always.*

I'm not 100 percent sure what God is saying to me, I'm afraid I'm going to take the wrong step." I understand this concern, but did you spot a certain word in there? "Afraid"? It is not the will of God for fear to rule in any area of your life—especially your walk with Him.

Don't be afraid to take a step because you think it will be the wrong one. God sees your heart. He knows that you are trying to please Him and live in obedience to His Word. He is not a cruel, angry God who is going to punish you if you take a misstep along the way. He sees your heart is right and you are trying to take a step toward His plan for your life—He is going to bless you for your desire to walk in your destiny. Take a step...God is waiting for you!

Just Start Walking

I think one of the best examples the Bible gives us of a person who took a step is Abraham. Abraham had a great call of God on his life—he was to be the "father of many nations" (Genesis 17:5)—but it didn't happen all at once. (As a matter of fact, anytime Abraham tried to make God's plan happen in his own strength, he got himself into trouble.) Abraham learned to simply take it one day at a time, obediently walking as the Lord led him. Look at what the author of Hebrews says about the way Abraham set out in pursuit of his new beginning:

> [Urged on] by faith Abraham, when he was called, obeyed and went forth to a place which he was destined to receive as an inheritance; and he went, although he did not know or trouble his mind about where he was to go.
>
> [Prompted] by faith he dwelt as a temporary resident in the land which was designated in the promise [of God, though he was like a stranger] in a strange country, living in tents with Isaac and Jacob, fellow heirs with him of the same promise.
>
> For he was [waiting expectantly and confidently] looking forward to the city which has fixed and firm foundations, whose Architect and Builder is God. (Hebrews 11:8–10)

Abraham's faith was marked by action. He didn't sit and wait for God to give him the entire plan. The Bible says that he started walking "although he did not know or trouble his mind about where he was to go." In other words, Abraham left the starting blocks—he didn't get stuck at "get set" just because he couldn't see the finish line. He wasn't sure exactly where he was going, and he wasn't sure exactly why he was going there. All he knew was that God told him to go in a certain direction, so Abraham took it one day at a time...one mile at a time...one step at a time.

Today, I believe that God wants to speak to us through Abraham's example. It's important that we not trouble ourselves trying to figure out the things God has yet to reveal. We may not know exactly where we're going or exactly how long it will take us to get there, but we still need to move in the direction God is calling us.

- You may not know how your finances are going to work out, but you feel God is telling you to give a certain amount to a hurting family in your neighborhood.
- You may not know for sure if you'll ever be in full-time ministry, but you feel God calling you to lead a Bible study at your church.
- You may not know how your marriage will ever heal, but you feel God is telling you to apologize to your spouse instead of demanding they apologize to you.
- You may not know how you could ever change your diet completely, but you can resist those sweets tonight.
- You may not know how you can ever fully forgive the person who hurt you so badly, but you feel God calling you to begin praying for them today.

That's how faith works. You take it one day at a time...one step at a time. You'd be surprised at what God can do when you are obedient with just one step. He can do more with your one step than you ever thought possible. And, eventually, as you begin to live out your faith one day at a time, the days start to pile up. At some point along the way, you look up and realize you aren't walking anymore, you're running—running in your destiny.

> *You'd be surprised at what God can do when you are obedient with just one step.*

Finding A Way To Buy Pencils

Linda Hernandez is a perfect example of someone who refused to get stuck at "get set." Instead, she took a step. She did something, even when it looked like the odds were stacked against her. I love her story—I think you will too.

Growing up in Lincoln, Nebraska, in the 1960s, Linda Hernandez recalls being part of one of the few Latino families in town, and that wasn't always easy. She told NPR's Story-Corps, "We had to sit in the back of the class, and stay after school and clean the erasers when the other kids didn't have to do that." Though Linda and her sister felt discriminated against, her parents wouldn't tolerate excuses and certainly wouldn't entertain the idea of withdrawing the kids from school. "Both my parents laid down the law and said, 'You have to go to school,'" Linda recalls.

When she was a junior in high school, Linda and her sister (a senior) faced an obstacle that many of us have never had to encounter. She spoke with her high school counselor about the annual achievement tests, but the counselor dismissed her inquiry. Linda was told that neither she nor her sister needed to concern themselves with the SAT Test or the ACT Test. Her counselor said that, because they were Hispanic women, "All you will do is have babies."

When Linda went home that afternoon and told her parents what the guidance counselor said, her mother went in the bedroom and cried. But her brother did something else. Linda recalls, "My brother said, 'Uh-uh, it ain't happening.' We were very lucky that he was over six feet tall. He walked us down to school and told our high school counselor, 'My sisters will take the test!'"

Linda and her sister were able to register to take the test, but they came up against another problem. They had to have #2 pencils to take the test, and they lived in such poverty that they didn't have the pencils needed for the test. Linda says she and her sister walked the alleys to collect soda bottles to turn in for a few cents a bottle. After a lot of work, they collected enough bottles to buy the pencils they needed.

Linda and her sister both scored extremely high on the test. Linda went on to college and her sister even received a four-year scholarship. Both earned their college degrees and had very successful careers. They faced the pressure of poverty and discrimination, but refused to give in to either "giant." When other people might have given up, Linda took a step. She took a step against discrimination. She took a step against poverty. They may have seemed like small steps at the time, but they sure paid off.

...GO!

I titled Section Two of this book *What's Stopping You?* because I believe it's important to make you aware of the things that will try to keep you miserably stuck in a life characterized by "too late"—too late for joy, too late for happiness, too late for peace in your family, too late for victory, and too late to see God's plan fulfilled.

Inaction is one of the main culprits. Inaction will anchor you to "too late" every single time. Fear, disbelief, worry, and anxiety will do everything they can to keep you stuck in the starting blocks of inaction while others run their race all around you. You may not know where the finish line is, and you may not know what will happen when you cross it, but—by the grace of God—you know how to take a step. And right now, that's all God is asking you to do.

The Bible tells us that God took the first steps. When we were far from Him, lost in our own sin, He sent Jesus (Romans 5:8). Stepping down from heaven, walking perfectly on this earth, and striding willingly to the cross, Jesus gave us what we could never earn on our own—the chance to experience God's eternity.

And now, with salvation available, the Bible shows us that anytime we step toward God, He steps toward us again. And His steps

> *Stepping down from heaven, walking perfectly on this earth, and striding willingly to the cross, Jesus gave us what we could never earn on our own—the chance to experience God's eternity.*

are much bigger than yours. As you give God your imperfect, flawed love, you receive His unconditional, perfect love in return. When you have faith as small as a mustard seed, God moves the mountains in your life. When you cast your cares on God, He gives you the peace that passes understanding.

Don't let the length of the journey intimidate you. Don't let the uncertainties of the terrain make you afraid. All you have to do is take the first step today. And if you're feeling nervous or unsure, listen carefully. You just might hear a voice from heaven encouraging you: *Go . . . Go . . . Go!*

God's been cheering you on the whole time.

Summary:

- In order to get to the finish line, you've got to leave the starting line.
- God unveils His plan in your life one step at a time.
- Faith is active, not passive. When you believe what God says, you do something about it.
- Don't let the fear of doing the wrong thing keep you from doing something.
- God took the first step toward you when He sent Jesus. He loves you more than you could ever know.

Action Steps You Can Take Today

Sometimes, when God begins to do a new work in our lives, we aren't sure what we're supposed to do to make it happen. But remember: it's not your job to make it happen—it's your job to take a step of faith. Not sure what those steps look like? Here are a few suggestions to get you started...

1. The "Prayer" Step

Prayer is one of the most important steps you can take. This is a way you can actively participate in faith each day. Thank God for what He is doing in your life; seek Him for His wisdom and guidance; be honest with Him about your doubts and concerns. Prayer isn't a last resort—prayer is the first step!

> *Do not fret or have anxiety about anything, but in every circumstance and in everything, by prayer and petition (definite requests), with thanksgiving, continue to make your wants known to God. (Philippians 4:6)*

> *Be unceasing in prayer [praying perseveringly]. (1 Thessalonians 5:17)*

2. The "Word" Step

I believe it is essential to begin each day in the Word of God. Reading, studying, and meditating on Scripture fills you with faith and gives you the strength you need for the challenges of the day. This is a powerful action step that will propel you into what God is calling you to do.

> *Your word is a lamp to my feet and a light to my path. (Psalm 119:105)*

> *For the Word that God speaks is alive and full of power [making it active, operative, energizing, and effective]; it is sharper*

117

*than any two-edged sword, penetrating to the dividing line of
the breath of life (soul) and [the immortal] spirit, and of joints
and marrow [of the deepest parts of our nature], exposing and
sifting and analyzing and judging the very thoughts and purposes of the heart. (Hebrews 4:12)*

3. The "Help Others" Step

Many times we are so busy trying to figure out how to help ourselves
that we never think to help others. In the midst of asking God what
He wants you to do today, find a way to help someone else. Being a
blessing to others is always the will of God, and this is a step that
you'll never regret. You may be surprised that as you look to meet the
needs of others, God will meet your needs along the way.

*Do not forget or neglect to do kindness and good, to be gener-
ous and distribute and contribute to the needy [of the church
as embodiment and proof of fellowship], for such sacrifices are
pleasing to God. (Hebrews 13:16)*

*Let each of you esteem and look upon and be concerned for not
[merely] his own interests, but also each for the interests of
others. (Philippians 2:4)*

4. The "Make A Choice" Step

The first step in doing anything is choosing to do it. In order to forgive, you first choose to forgive. In order to be at peace, you first
choose not to worry. In order to start something new, you first choose
to step out and go for it. You may not know how it's all going to work
out, but you can make some foundational choices today. It's as simple as
saying to yourself, "Today I choose peace over worry! Today I choose
to break that old habit! Today I choose not to lash out in anger!" Make
a choice; take a step today, and never forget to ask for God's help
(His grace) in executing your choice. We can do all things with and

through Him, but we can do nothing without Him (John 15:5; Philippians 4:13).

> ... Then choose for yourselves this day whom you will serve. (Joshua 24:15 NIV)

> ... I have set before you life and death, the blessings and the curses; therefore choose life, that you and your descendants may live. (Deuteronomy 30:19)

5. The "Thanksgiving" Step

One of the best ways to enjoy your life is to stop and thank God for the good things He has given you. Sometimes we are so anxious to get something new from God that we aren't enjoying the things He has already blessed us with. When you aren't sure what step to take, I encourage you to take the "thanksgiving" step. Actively thank God for His kindness, His goodness, and His faithfulness in your life. You'll be amazed at how this action will change your perspective and affect your day.

> Thank [God] in everything [no matter what the circumstances may be, be thankful and give thanks], for this is the will of God for you [who are] in Christ Jesus [the Revealer and Mediator of that will]. (1 Thessalonians 5:18)

> At all times and for everything giving thanks in the name of our Lord Jesus Christ to God the Father. (Ephesians 5:20)

IT'S NEVER TOO LATE TO . . .

✓ Get Out Of Debt

✓ Step Out Of Your Comfort Zone

✓ Look Forward

✓ Get Unstuck

✓ Invest In Someone Other Than Yourself

✓ Make Right Choices / Do The Right Thing

✓ Say "Thank You"

✓ Be Inspired

✓ Know You Have Been Forgiven

✓ Learn A New Skill

✓ Give And Receive Love

✓ Start Living Healthfully

✓ Begin An Adventure

✓ Enjoy Your Life

✓ Reunite Your Family

✓ Be The Spiritual Leader God Has Called You To Be

Today Is Your Day

Behold, the fresh and new has come!

2 Corinthians 5:17; Part III

CHAPTER 11

Little Things Make A Big Difference

*"Be faithful in small things because it is in them that your
strength lies."*

—Mother Teresa

For years, Danny Cahill led a destructive life of addictive behavior.
He smoked two packs of cigarettes a day, engaged in chronic binge
eating, and gambled compulsively. His wife, Darci, said that Danny
became angry, unhappy, and secluded. Darci didn't know how to
help. She confessed, "I felt lost."

Eventually, Danny's actions began to affect his health and his
family—his weight rose to 460 pounds, and he ran up $45,000 in
credit card debt. There seemed to be no end in sight. Darci says that
at first, she tried to fix things in her own strength. She remembers
praying, "Lord, throw me a bone here. I've got to know what to do."
But she felt the Lord saying to her, *Trust Me, and give [Danny] to Me.
He's not your responsibility.* From that point on, Darci began to pray
that God would speak directly to Danny so that real change would
take place.

And that's exactly what happened. The Lord began to show Danny
how his actions were affecting his family. Danny said, "All those
things that I didn't see before, now I saw. It was like: 'Danny, *your*
lack of self-control and *your* undisciplined life are affecting every-

thing around you, especially your children who model everything you do." With this new realization, Danny stopped gambling, but his debt was overwhelming. He and Darci prayed that God would give them a sign and tell them what to do.

That very night they went to a church service where I happened to be the guest speaker. Of course, I didn't know them or know anything about their story, but in my message that night, I said the following thing:

> *"The Bible tells us we need to confront issues. Some of you are trying to get away from some things that you need to go through. Anytime you're running from something or hiding from something, it has power and authority over you."*

That service was a turning point for Danny. He said, "It was like a light switch was turned on." That night, he faced his problems and started making healthy decisions that would affect his future. But lasting change didn't happen overnight—it happened through a series of small decisions and daily disciplines. Danny observed, "You don't just jump out of a hole. You have to create a plan and take it one step at a time. It might take a thousand steps, but with every one step you're closer to the end." So Danny went about the process of taking those "thousand steps." Over the next couple of years, he and Darci started to incrementally and strategically move toward their goal. Danny faithfully worked a second job, making regular payments against their financial burden. Eventually, he eliminated the credit card debt that once threatened to overwhelm him.

But there is something else about Danny that makes his story unique. If the name Danny Cahill is familiar to you, it's because Danny applied for and was accepted on the weight-loss television show, *The Biggest Loser*. Throughout season eight of the NBC hit show, he applied his one-step-at-a-time attitude toward his weight-loss goals. Danny Cahill won that season of *The Biggest Loser* by losing more weight than anyone had ever lost until that season—239 pounds!

It didn't happen overnight. Danny said, "I did it through hard work, not giving up, and knowing that each step led me to that end point." And the best part of it all is that Danny now travels all over the country telling people his story and sharing his faith in God.

Small Beginnings

I think there is something really powerful about Danny's story. But to be honest, I know it will be tempting to focus on *$45,000 paid off* and *239 pounds lost*. Those are the attention grabbers, aren't they? Those are the big numbers that get people talking. I understand that, but those aren't the really important numbers. Do you know what the important numbers are? Let me tell you:

1…2…3…4…5…

If you think about it, that's how Danny paid off his debt, and that's how Danny lost the weight.

- Working *one hour at a time* at his second job.
- Making *one payment at a time* toward his mountain of debt.
- Losing *one or two or three pounds at a time* through hard work and sacrifice.
- Exercising *one day at a time* to get healthy.
- And NEVER GIVING UP!

The big numbers aren't reached unless the small numbers are realized. The *$45,000* and *239 pounds* don't happen unless *1, 2,* and *3* happen first. Small beginnings are the launching pad to great endings.

This is a truth that can be difficult for us to accept in today's culture. We're fascinated with the

> *Small beginnings are the launching pad to great endings.*

idea of instant results. Our motto could be: BIGGER, *Faster!!!* We don't have to look too hard to see this motto in action: Athletes bulk up with steroids rather than trusting their training regimen; hopeful ticket holders aim for wealth through state lotteries rather than investing in solid financial planning; talent show contestants dream of becoming music sensations overnight rather than paying their dues in a competitive industry. In our quest for BIGGER, *Faster!!!*, we have forgotten about the importance and value of small beginnings.

The Bible talks a lot about small beginnings. God is a big God—and He can certainly do things quickly when He wants to—but usually, He will develop things in our lives through small steps. He starts small and works up to larger things, all the while helping us handle the increasing responsibilities and opportunities. Look at what these verses say about small beginnings:

> *Do not despise these small beginnings, for the Lord rejoices to see the work begin . . . (Zechariah 4:10 NLT)*

> *And though your beginning was small, yet your latter end would greatly increase. (Job 8:7)*

> *". . . I tell you the truth, if you had faith even as small as a mustard seed, you could say to this mountain, 'Move from here to there,' and it would move. Nothing would be impossible." (Matthew 17:20 NLT)*

> Some of the deepest, richest things God does in your life begin on a small scale—a small prompting, a small decision, a small blessing.

Some of the deepest, richest things God does in your life begin on a small scale—a small prompting, a small decision, a small blessing. It might not impress a television audience, and confetti might not fall from the sky when it happens, but that little thing that God is speaking to your heart is of utmost importance in your relationship with Him. *New* beginnings usually start with *small* beginnings. Dare to believe today that it's not too late for you to begin!

The Value of Small Beginnings

Now, I'm not writing about small beginnings to discourage you. This is news that I hope will do the exact opposite—you should be greatly encouraged! That small decision you made today to hold your tongue...that may be part of a larger thing God is teaching you about self-control. That small effort you made this morning to bless a neighbor...that may have a larger impact than you ever realized. That small decision not to make the purchase you wanted and knew you didn't need...that may be the first of many financial breakthroughs. That small amount of self-control you displayed at lunch when you ordered a healthier option...that may be the first step down the road to a larger victory. When you are living for God, small beginnings are simply miracles in seed form.

I understand that it can be frustrating when you see a coworker advancing more rapidly than you, or when you have to listen to a relative brag about how quickly they've achieved success. Sometimes going two steps forward and one step back seems like a painfully slow process. However, you don't know how long it really took them to get to where they are now, and you also don't know how long their success is going to last. Sadly, many things that rise quickly fall just as quickly. They look amazing, but no one took the time to lay a strong foundation of faith, integrity, and character. Don't waste time being jealous of, or comparing your life to, someone else. As my husband, Dave, always says, "Slow and steady, fast and fragile."

I want you to know that God has a wonderful plan for your life. If you submit your heart to Him and give Him permission to have

His way in your life, He is going to do something amazing. You will never feel left out, left behind, or forgotten. God's work always accomplishes *more* than you imagined, and this work always happens in His perfect timing! When you decide to make a beginning, always remember that it will take time to get to the end. Be a finisher in life!!

Let me point out the beauty of the small things God is doing in your life:

1. Small Things Let You Practice For Bigger Things

There are no overnight sensations in the kingdom of God. What God shows us by revelation is finished through implementation. The things He is doing in your life right now have a twofold purpose: they are providing for you today, and they are preparing you for tomorrow.

I am blessed to travel the world, preaching to auditoriums full of people, but I didn't start that way. I started out in ministry by teaching a home Bible study. And you know what? I poured my heart into that Bible study in the same way I pour my heart into preaching to crowds of thousands. God did some amazing things in those early Bible studies, and (though I didn't know it at the time) one of those things was preparing me for what was to come.

Consider this: David's encounter with the lion and the bear prepared him for his battle against Goliath. Joseph learned how to lead in an Egyptian prison, taking lessons he would use when he was second only to Pharaoh. The disciples helped control the crowds when Jesus taught, but one day they would preach to crowds in His name.

Don't be in such a hurry. If you go too fast, you will miss important lessons that come through the seemingly small decisions and events of each new day lived in relationship with the Lord. God is doing valuable things in our lives every day and we need to learn to recognize them.

2. Small Things Prove Your Character

For most of us, if God gave us everything we were asking for all at once, it would crush us. Our character simply wouldn't be strong enough to handle the responsibility that comes with the level of authority we desire. This is why God gives us small responsibilities first—He uses them to develop and prove our character.

If you are praying for the finances so you can go back to school, God may provide the money for only one or two classes. Don't be frustrated. Learn the lessons about studying and time management on this level so that you will be ready for a busier schedule later. When God has taught you what you need to learn, and when you have embraced what He has given you, He'll release more.

> *When God has taught you what you need to learn, and when you have embraced what He has given you, He'll release more.*

If you have a dream to start a charity that reaches families all over the country, God will probably give you opportunities to help families in your own neighborhood. There are lessons to be learned there, trust to be earned, and credibility to be established. When you have served faithfully on one level, God will open the door to the next level.

Remember what Jesus taught in the Parable of the Talents:

> *His master said to him, Well done, you upright (honorable, admirable) and faithful servant! You have been faithful and trustworthy over a little; I will put you in charge of much. (Matthew 25:21)*

3. Small Things Pile Up

Danny's story was a perfect example of this truth. Small things stacked upon each other lead to big victories. Instead of letting the enemy discourage you because you can't reach your ultimate goal in one day, encourage yourself by accomplishing small, reachable goals every day of the week.

- You may not be able to lose 50 pounds in one day, but you can work to lose one pound a week for 50 weeks.
- You may not be able to fix your marriage in one day, but you can choose to do one thing each day to be a better spouse.
- You may not be able to read the whole Bible in one day, but you can decide to read one or two chapters a day.
- You may not be able to undo every bad habit in one day, but you can stop one bad habit today by starting a good habit.

Build a personal portfolio of good decisions, smart choices, healthy attitudes, joyful mind-sets, encouraging conversations, and peaceful afternoons. When you look at each of these decisions on an individual basis, they may seem small and insignificant, but these God-honoring actions are piling up. You may not realize it, but God is doing something new and revolutionary in your life...one small choice at a time.

Yeah, But It's Only...

In Mark chapter 6, the crowd that Jesus was ministering to grew hungry. (Some theologians estimate this crowd of 5,000 men to be as large as 15,000 total people.) He was teaching in a "desolate and isolated" place, so the disciples urged Jesus to send the crowd away so they would have time to make it back to their homes and get something to eat. But Jesus had a better plan in mind. (Side note: Jesus' plan is always better than our plan.) He said:

"How many loaves do you have? Go and see." (Mark 6:38)

Jesus wanted the disciples to take action—to *do* something. The disciples reported that they had only five loaves of bread and two fish. And John's account of the same story tells us that the bread and fish were from the lunch of a *"little boy"* (John 6:9). You probably know the rest of the story: Jesus took the five loaves and two fish, blessed them, and miraculously fed the crowd with plenty to spare.

If you have been a Christian for a long period of time, you may have heard that story hundreds of times, but there is an important application here for you today: With God, there is no such thing as "only" or "not enough."

NOT ENOUGH PEOPLE HAD FOOD TO GIVE? NO PROBLEM!

HE WAS ONLY A LITTLE BOY? PERFECT!

THERE WERE ONLY FIVE LOAVES OF BREAD AND NOT ENOUGH FISH? MORE THAN ENOUGH!

Jesus took their *not enough* and turned it into His *more than enough*. What they had didn't seem adequate, but they gave it to Jesus and He made it astounding.

I believe He wants to do the same thing in your life. As a child of God, there is no such thing as *only* or *not enough*. You may think, "I don't have enough talent, the *only* thing I know how to do is…" or, "I didn't accomplish everything I wanted for the Lord today. The *only* thing I did was…" or maybe even, "I can't think of much to be joyful about today. The *only* thing I can think of is so small that it is not enough."

God looks at your *only* or *not enough* and says, *No problem! Perfect! More than enough!*

Those small things that seem insignificant to you are infinite in

> *God can take your **only** and turn it into His **plenty!***

the hands of God. He can do a miracle with every little thing you give Him. God can take your *only* and turn it into His *plenty*!

There is nothing too small to give to God. Each seed you sow, each decision that you make for Him on a daily basis, will reap a plentiful harvest. Like Danny Cahill discovered, your one-step-at-a-time attitude can deeply affect your life and the lives of all those around you. Make the decision today that *"Yeah, but it's only…"* is a phrase you never have to use again.

One Starfish At A Time

Loren Eiseley tells a story that shows us the importance of a small beginning:

> *While wandering a deserted beach at dawn, stagnant in my work, I saw a man in the distance bending and throwing as he walked the endless stretch toward me. As he came near, I could see that he was throwing starfish, abandoned on the sand by the tide, back into the sea.*
>
> *When he was close enough, I asked him why he was working so hard at this strange task. He said that the sun would dry the starfish and they would die. I said to him that I thought he was foolish. There were thousands of starfish on miles and miles of beach. One man alone could never make a difference. He smiled as he picked up the next starfish. Hurling it far into the sea he said, "It makes a difference for this one."*
>
> *I abandoned my writing and spent the morning throwing starfish.*

I encourage you today: You are making a bigger impact than you know. Don't despise the day of small beginnings. The little bit you have—time, talent, energy, understanding, obedience—is more than enough in the hands of God. Don't be discouraged or grow impatient. Beginning again is rarely a huge, cataclysmic event. Beginning again is a disciplined, faithful, step-by-step process. Sometimes you have to begin again today...

and tomorrow...

and the day after that...

and the day after that.

With the help of the Lord, these daily decisions are leading you into a brand-new life in God. All you have to do is stay faithful and refuse to give up. As a matter of fact, refusing to give up is what the next chapter in this book is all about.

Summary:

- Sometimes the most important number is "one"—one step at a time.
- Small beginnings are miracles in seed form.
- The Lord will always give you an opportunity to prove faithful over little before He puts you in charge of much (Matthew 25:21).
- God can do a miracle with every little thing you give Him.
- Beginning again with God is a disciplined, faithful, step-by-step process.

> *"There are many of us that are willing to do great things for the Lord, but few of us are willing to do little things."*
> —Dwight L. Moody

CHAPTER 12

Quitting Isn't An Option

"The best way out is always through."

—Robert Frost

Grandma Cha Sa-soon, known as Ms. Cha, is one of the most unlikely national heroes South Korea has ever known. She isn't famous for a particular talent. She's never run for public office. She's not an actress, a musician, or a pop star. She's just persistent. Very, very persistent.

Ms. Cha is famous for passing her driver's license test...on her 950th try.

Born into an extremely poor family in the mountain village of Sinchon, South Korea, Ms. Cha and her six siblings spent their childhood working in the nearby fields to help earn money for the family. She attended an informal night school when time allowed, but she didn't have the opportunity to register in a formal day school until she was 15 years old. She began classes as a fourth grader, but didn't advance much further. "Middle school was just a dream for me," she would later say.

Ms. Cha spent her life taking the bus, but she always envied people who could drive. There were times she would miss the bus and have to wait two hours for the next one. This was a frustrating inconvenience, and though she was now in her 60s, Ms. Cha decided it was time to get her driver's license.

When asked why she didn't try to get her license earlier in life, she responded, "I was too busy raising my four children. Eventually they all grew up and went away, and my husband died several years ago, and I had more time for myself. I wanted to get a driver's license so I could take my grandchildren to the zoo." Many people would think that at this stage of life, it was too late to do such a thing, but not Ms. Cha.

Because of her lack of education, the written test proved to be a difficult obstacle. The test was a 50-minute test, consisting of 40 multiple-choice questions pertaining to road regulations and car maintenance, but much of the terminology confused her. Even when she could read the words, she didn't always comprehend what they meant. However, she refused to give up, waking up at 4 a.m. each day to study the worn and tattered pages of her test preparation books.

Every day, she took two buses to the test site, which was an hour away, and every day she failed the test. She failed it the first time... and the 10th time...and the 50th time...and the 100th time...and the 500th time. One teacher at a local driving school that tried to help Ms. Cha along the way said, "It drove you crazy to teach her, but we could not get mad at her. She was always cheerful. She still had the spirit of a little girl in her."

Finally, in November 2009, on her 950th try, Ms. Cha passed her written test. Later, she passed both of her driving skills and road tests. To the rousing cheers of instructors and agency officials, Grandma Cha Sa-soon was awarded her hard-earned driver's license.

When asked about her dogged determination, Park Seong-ju, her 36-year-old son, said, "Mother has lived a hard life, selling vegetables door to door and working other people's farms. Maybe that made her stubborn. If she puts her mind to something, no one can argue her out of it."

One visit to Ms. Cha's house confirms that her son is right. On her wall, beside black-and-white pictures of her and her late husband as a young couple is a handwritten sign. Translated, the sign simply reads, "Never give up!"

The Battle Is The Lord's

I believe one of the most important traits a Christian can have is determination. A persistent Christian is a prepared and powerful Christian. Persistence is key because there are going to be difficulties in life. The Bible never promised that when you gave your life to God, you'd no longer have any problems. As I'm sure you've noticed, life isn't always a cakewalk; there are going to be difficult days and trying circumstances, but going through them instead of giving up is what makes us strong.

When you know who you are in God and trust the power of the Holy Spirit within you, you don't give up when things get tough—you persevere. You don't panic and

> *A persistent Christian is a prepared and powerful Christian.*

succumb to discouragement just because you failed a test once or twice (or 949 times). Instead, you trust that God is in control, and you ask Him to give you the strength that you need to carry on.

I just started working with a new strength training coach, and he told me that when I got to repetition 9 or 10, if I felt the weight I was lifting was going to be too much, I could use my own discretion about when to stop. I told him that if the goal was 10, I would do 10 if there was any possible way for me to do it. I said, "If I quit early, you can be guaranteed that I absolutely could not go on." I wasn't bragging; that is just the way I am. I had to make that decision early in life when I was being abused and no adult was willing to help me. I had to make it again when my first husband walked out on me when I was pregnant so he could live with another woman. I had to make it again when God called me into ministry and I was asked to leave my church, resulting in me losing all of my friends. When my strength was gone, I finally realized I needed to rely on God's strength all along.

Perhaps the reason God didn't rescue me from all these difficulties was for the purpose of building that determination in me—because without it, none of us can do anything great in life. If you have big dreams, then you will need determination!

Galatians 6:9 is a very important and encouraging verse about persistence. It says:

> And let us not lose heart and grow weary and faint in acting nobly and doing right, for in due time and at the appointed season we shall reap, if we do not loosen and relax our courage and faint.

The apostle Paul, under the divine inspiration of the Holy Spirit, is telling us something crucial about our walk with God: You will see victory *if* you don't give up. In other words, the only way you can lose is if you stop fighting. That's a promise worth getting excited about! Your problem can't defeat you. The devil can't defeat you. Fear can't defeat you. You can overcome every obstacle, as long as you refuse to give up, because you have the Spirit of God inside of you.

You can overcome every obstacle, as long as you refuse to give up, because you have the Spirit of God inside of you.

I wish more people understood the power of godly determination. I hear from individuals all the time who have given up. The battle got too intense—the test seemed too hard—and somewhere along the way, they just stopped fighting. Like Peter who put his focus on the wind and the waves instead of Jesus, they've put their focus on the turmoil in their lives instead of Jesus, and it has caused them to become afraid. Maybe you know exactly what I'm talking about.

Maybe you're overwhelmed and exhausted, and you're tempted to give up.

If that's you, I want you to know that I understand what you're going through. I may not have gone through your exact situation, but I know what it's like to be tempted to give up. There have been plenty of times in my life when I've felt exhausted, wondering how I would ever find the strength to keep going.

Usually when I feel that way it's because I'm trying to fight the battle in my own strength. I'm spending the day worrying about the problem, constantly talking about the issue and trying to come up with my own plan to fix it. *Does any of that sound familiar?*

Anytime I feel that way—overwhelmed and tempted to give up—the Lord reminds me that He has promised to fight my battles for me. I'm not called to win in my own strength—He wins in His strength. I need to bring that problem to God and lay it at His feet. The Bible reminds us time and time again that God goes before us, and the battle belongs to Him . . .

> *The Lord says this to you: Be not afraid or dismayed at this great multitude; for the battle is not yours, but God's.* (2 Chronicles 20:15)

> *"Not by might nor by power, but by my Spirit," says the Lord Almighty.* (Zechariah 4:6 NIV)

> *. . . With us is the Lord our God to help us and to fight our battles . . .* (2 Chronicles 32:8)

These are the promises that we need to hold on to when we begin to feel like throwing in the towel. Perseverance is never about confidence and determination that *you* have the strength to win; it is always about confidence and determination that *God* has the strength to win. Instead of praying, "Lord, I don't know how I'm going to do this," pray, "Lord, I can't wait to see how You're going to do this."

When you begin to trust that the battle is the Lord's, the way you view your problem will completely change.

Just ask a guy named Gehazi. He knows all about it...

Those With Us Are More Than Those With Them

In 2 Kings chapter 6, it doesn't look good for the prophet Elisha and his servant, Gehazi. Well, at least not to Gehazi.

Elisha was warning the king of Israel about the Syrian army's troop movements. In his prayer time, Elisha heard God telling him where the enemy army was gathering, and Elisha sent word to the king. This resulted in "repeated" victories for the people of God (v. 10).

The king of Syria was so baffled by the perfect placement of the Israelite army, he was convinced there was a traitor in his midst who was feeding information to the enemy. When he interrogated his servants, they assured him no one was selling secrets to the Israelites, but that the prophet Elisha was the one helping the Israelites. Upon hearing this news, the king of Syria was determined to kill Elisha. Verse 14 tells us he sent "horses, chariots, and a great army" by night to surround the city where Elisha lived.

This brings us back to poor Gehazi.

When Gehazi got up early the next morning and went outside, he was terrified to see the Syrian army surrounding the city. The Bible tells us he cried out, "Alas, my master! What shall we do?" (v. 15). (Have you ever felt that way? Have you ever looked at a circumstance that seems to have you surrounded on every side and wondered, "What am I going to do?")

But Elisha wasn't in panic mode like Gehazi seemed to be. Instead, he confidently said to the servant, "Fear not; for those with us are more than those with them" (v. 16). Gehazi didn't know what Elisha meant by that. I can just picture him looking at his master and then looking at himself and thinking, "I count two people. You and me." They were no match for the army of chariots surrounding them.

> *Then Elisha prayed, Lord, I pray You, open his eyes that he may see. And the Lord opened the young man's eyes, and he saw, and behold, the mountain was full of horses and chariots of fire round about Elisha. (2 Kings 6:17)*

Elisha saw what Gehazi didn't—the battle was the Lord's. He knew that they had no chance in their own strength, but they weren't called to fight in their strength. God was present to give them the victory. Before Gehazi realized that, he was stuck in fear, ready to raise the white flag of surrender. But the moment Gehazi got a heavenly perspective and saw that God was present to win the battle, nothing in the world could have talked him into quitting. The battle was over before it even began.

Refuse To Give Up

Like Elisha, I pray that God will open your eyes today. I know that the battle you're going through isn't easy. I understand the situation surrounding you looks intimidating. And I realize sometimes quitting seems like the best option. If you only see what Gehazi first saw, your situation might seem hopeless.

But there is a greater truth for you today. "Fear not; for those with us are more than those with them." God is fighting on your behalf. He sees your situation. He knows exactly what you're going through. He promises to never leave you or forsake you.

The only way you can lose is if you quit, so today I want to encourage you: No matter what happens, no matter what it looks like in the

> *Sometimes the most spiritual thing you can say is, "I'm not going to give up!"*

natural, no matter what lie the enemy tries to tell you...REFUSE
TO GIVE UP. Sometimes the most spiritual thing you can say is,
"I'm not going to give up! God promised to fight my battles for me,
so I'm going to be obedient, walk in faith, and wait for His victory.
But I REFUSE TO GIVE UP!"

When people say bad things about you... *refuse to give up.*
When it looks impossible... *refuse to give up.*
When things appear to get worse instead of better... *refuse to
give up.*
When you fail the test 949 times... *refuse to give up.*

When you persevere, you'll find that God has been in control the
entire time. He's been teaching you, providing for you, and preparing you all along. God can use every challenge you've outlasted for
your good.

Summary:

- A persistent Christian is a prepared and powerful Christian.
- You only lose if you give up.
- Rely on God's strength (not your own). He has promised to
  fight your battle for you.
- Fear makes you feel surrounded by an enemy. Faith makes you
  realize you are surrounded by God.
- A great prayer to pray is, "Lord, open my eyes so that I may see
  that those with us are more than those with them."

Persistence Pays Off

Beethoven handled the violin awkwardly and preferred playing his own compositions instead of improving his technique. His teacher called him hopeless as a composer.

When General Douglas MacArthur applied for admission to West Point, he was turned down not once, but twice. He tried a third time, was accepted, and marched into the history books.

When the first *Chicken Soup for the Soul* book was completed, it was turned down by 33 publishers in New York and another 90 at the American Booksellers Association convention in Anaheim, California. The major New York publishers said, "It is too nicey-nice," and "Nobody wants to read a book of short little stories." Since that time, more than eight million copies of the original *Chicken Soup for the Soul* book have been sold.

In 1954, Jimmy Denny, manager of the Grand Ole Opry, fired Elvis Presley after one performance. He told Presley, "You ain't goin' nowhere...son. You ought to go back to drivin' a truck." Elvis Presley went on to become the most popular singer in America.

Dr. Seuss's first children's book, *And to Think That I Saw It on Mulberry Street*, was rejected by 27 publishers. The 28th publisher, Vanguard Press, sold six million copies of the book.

Stories compiled from *Chicken Soup for the Writer's Soul* and *A Cup of Chicken Soup for the Soul*.

CHAPTER 13

Don't Waste Your Mistakes

"The world breaks everyone and afterward many are stronger at the broken places."

—Ernest Hemingway

"But do I HAVE to eat my vegetables? I hate vegetables!"

If you've navigated the waters of parenthood, you've probably heard that question and declaration a time or two. Not all kids hate all vegetables, but they all seem to go through a phase when they don't like a particular vegetable…and it's usually the one you chose to put on their plate. Carrots, peas, beans, broccoli, asparagus—you name it, they don't want to eat it.

One of my grandsons went through a long phase in which he would only eat plain noodles (and I do mean *plain*—no butter, no oil, no sauce, no salt) and yogurt and green beans. That was it… he wouldn't eat anything else. As my daughter-in-law checked with other parents, she discovered that many of them had experienced their child going through some very "picky" stages of eating. I believe as Christians we are the same way on our journey of spiritual growth.

A wise parent will teach their children at an early age the importance of a balanced and nutritious diet, and God is trying to teach us in the same way. When kids learn to appreciate healthy choices early in life, it makes for a much healthier transition into adulthood.

If you didn't grow up with nutritious options, you know how difficult it can be to appreciate the proper foods and to correct improper eating habits later in life. Though vegetables aren't as fun to eat as cupcakes, they're important for your body. And that's why you have probably looked at your children and said something like this a time or two (or 200): "You need to at least take a few bites."

You may be thinking, "Joyce, why are you talking about vegetables and cupcakes? You're making me hungry!" Well, this chapter isn't about nutrition (if this is a topic that interests you, I suggest you read my book *Look Great, Feel Great: 12 Keys to Enjoying a Healthy Life Now*), but there is a connection I want you to see. I think our mistakes and failures are similar to vegetables—the things on our plate that can be good for us, but we'd rather do without. The trials and tribulations in life are the same way. We don't want them, but they do help make us strong as we exercise our faith in God all the way through them.

The mistakes and failures we've made in the past—whether they happened 10 years ago or 10 minutes ago—can help us grow if we bring them to the Lord and ask Him what we can learn from the experience. We can choose to use them (learn from them), or we can choose to waste them (regret them, feel guilty, and get stuck in them). When it comes to your mistakes, I want to encourage you: Don't waste anything on your plate.

> *The mistakes and failures we've made in the past—whether they happened 10 years ago or 10 minutes ago—can help us grow if we bring them to the Lord and ask Him what we can learn from the experience.*

Let Your Mistakes Be Your Teacher

God doesn't want you to live stuck in your past. The apostle Paul famously said, "... forgetting what lies behind and straining forward to what lies ahead, I press on..." (Philippians 3:13–14). Paul made a decision not to live stuck in the mistakes of his past, but that doesn't mean he didn't remember his mistakes and learn from them. Paul knew how destructive the legalism and works-based religion was that he had been stuck in before he met Jesus, so he learned from that and never went back to his old way of life again. And he spent his entire ministry teaching others the truth of salvation by the grace of God, through faith in Jesus.

Sadly, many people today continue to fall back into the mistakes and patterns of their past. They keep going around the same mountain, time and time again, having to learn the same lesson multiple times. Wisdom is learning from your mistakes and moving on. You don't have to be a repeat offender—you can have victory once and for all! In the judicial system, being a three-time loser, or someone who has repeated the same offense three times, is a serious problem. It often means life in prison. Thank God for His mercy and the opportunity to begin again no matter how many times we have made mistakes in the past. We don't have to live our lives in the prison of regret, guilt, and failure because we have made some mistakes. Jesus came to open prison doors and set captives free (Isaiah 61:1).

Let's say you lost your temper and yelled at your kids or your spouse four times today. Well, that was a mistake. It's not God's best, and you probably felt the conviction of the Holy Spirit the moment it happened. You have a choice to make. You can either...

A. Be Condemned For Your Mistake

This is the enemy's plan for your life. He wants to make you feel terrible about yourself because of your failure. Condemnation is different from conviction. Conviction is the Holy Spirit showing you when you've done something wrong and helping you get back to the place you need to be. Conviction corrects the failure and reminds you that God's grace is available for you. Condemnation is full of shame. It makes you think that you are terrible, and it tries to tell you God is angry with you.

Don't allow the enemy to bring condemnation into your life. When you sin, take it to God and receive His forgiveness. Remember, Romans 8:1 says, "Therefore, [there is] now no condemnation (no adjudging guilty of wrong) for those who are in Christ Jesus…"

B. Be Glad You're Forgiven, But Don't Bother To Learn Anything

This is the response of your flesh. Just as you acted out in the flesh (and we all have those moments when this happens), your flesh is not interested in learning anything. It is lazy and has no interest in discipline. If we don't take our mistake seriously and truly desire to turn away from it (repent), we are likely to do it again.

I've heard it said that insanity is doing the same thing over and over again, but expecting a different result. If you neglect to learn from your failure, you're setting yourself up to fail again; but this isn't God's plan for your life. He is greater than that mistake, and He wants you to walk in victory over it. Anger is not stronger than God. Worry is not stronger than God. Fear is not stronger than God. An addiction is not stronger than God. You can bring any sin and failure to Him and live in His power to overcome it.

C. Take Your Mistake To God And Ask Him To Forgive You And Teach You From It

Just because you lost your temper yesterday doesn't mean you are destined to live a life blowing up at people all the time. Actually, the fact that you lost your temper yesterday can be the catalyst for change in your life. If you'll go to the Lord and say, "Lord, I know that was a mistake, and I don't want to live that way. I realize that my anger hurts the people I love. Please help me learn from it, and please help me today so that I won't repeat that failure. Lord, show me how to respond differently," God will answer that prayer. He will teach you what you need to learn through that failure. Your progress may be slow at first, but if you won't give up, you will reach your goal!

In the future when you feel that same temptation to lose your temper, you will be ready to resist it with the power of the Holy Spirit. You're dressed in God's armor, you're a veteran of previous battles, and you're wiser than before. This is the value of learning from yesterday's mistakes.

Learn From The Mistakes Of Others

People say to me all the time, "Joyce, I can't believe you tell some of the stories you tell. You're so open and vulnerable about your own personal struggles in life. I don't know if I could stand up there and share some of the things you share." It's true, I do tell people about my own issues. I talk about my arguments with Dave, the insecurities I've had to overcome, the way I used to worry about everything, and a whole host of other issues God has brought me through over the years.

I share these things because I believe they might prevent others from going through some of the same struggles that I went through. If you can learn through a sermon what I had to learn through a struggle, you've saved some time and some heartache. Now, there will be some things that you can learn only firsthand, but there are many other things you can learn if you'll just pay attention to what God may be saying to you through the lives of people around you.

You don't have to perpetuate cycles of sin or dysfunction that you've seen in your family. You can break those cycles—generational curses can stop with you.

I suggest you pray and ask the Holy Spirit to help you avoid the same mistakes that you saw your parents, your friends, or your relatives make. You don't have to perpetuate cycles of sin or dysfunction that you've seen in your family. You can break those cycles—generational curses can stop with you.

- Just because your father was a certain way, or your mother was a certain way, doesn't mean you have to be that way. Say: "Lord, I'm going to learn from their failure. With Your help, my life is going to be different."
- Just because your coworkers are all gossiping about a certain situation doesn't mean you have to fall into the same trap. Say: "Lord, I see how they talk and I also notice they are never joyful. I'm going to learn from that and refuse to participate. With Your help, I'm going to resist that temptation."
- Just because your friends spend their days stressed out and worried about their lives doesn't mean you have to do the same thing. Say: "Lord, I see the damage that stress and worry can bring. I know Your presence brings peace and joy. With Your help, I refuse to live worried and stressed about situations beyond my control."

Many years ago Dave and I took a nine-month Bible school program at a church we were attending. We were hungry to learn, and we sacrificed two evenings a week at home in order to go to the school. This was especially challenging for Dave after working at his job all day, but we were anxious to learn, so we went. We did learn a lot, but not in the way we expected. We actually witnessed some very bad behavior by some of the leadership, and it ended up teaching us "what not to do in ministry." It ended up being a lesson that stayed with us for life, and we have been better people because of it.

> *If you'll be observant and learn from the mistakes of others, I believe God will help you avoid the same mistakes yourself.*

If you'll be observant and learn from the mistakes of others, I believe God will help you avoid the same mistakes yourself. Don't judge them critically for their mistakes, and don't gossip about them, but pray for them and determine that those mistakes will be a learning experience for you.

Learn From The Mistakes People Made In The Bible

The Bible is the infallible, perfect Word of God, but it is full of fallible, imperfect people. Isn't it encouraging to know that the men and women in the Bible weren't all some sort of superheroes? They were real people with real problems just like you and me. *David got discouraged. Moses lacked confidence. Elijah got depressed. Gideon was afraid. Sarah laughed in disbelief at God's promise. The Israelites rebelled. Zacchaeus was too short. The crowd got hungry. Martha didn't get her house cleaned in time and she resented that her sister Mary wasn't working as hard as she was. Peter denied Christ. The disciples slept when they should have been praying.* The Bible is full of relatable people who made human mistakes. The good news is we don't have to make the same mistakes—we can learn from their stories in God's Word!

In 1 Corinthians 10, Paul is talking about the failures of the Israelites in the wilderness and he says: "Now these things are examples (warnings and admonitions) for us..." (v. 6) and he goes on to say, "Now these things befell them by way of a figure [as an example and warning to us]; they were written to admonish and fit us for right action by good instruction..." (v. 11). Paul is saying in no uncertain terms that we have the opportunity to learn from the stories we read in the Bible.

We can glean instruction from the victories and successes of God's people in the Word, but we can also learn from their struggles and failures. When we see Abraham and Sarah trying to make God's promise come true in their own strength, we can learn from that and patiently wait on the Lord. When we see the Israelites demand to have a king in order to be like every other nation around them, we can learn the importance of following God and refusing to follow the crowd. When we see the rich young ruler walk away from Jesus because he didn't want to part with his wealth, we can learn about the dangers of putting possessions and material things before the Lord.

These are stories with incredible value to the life of the believer. Each time you read the Word, I encourage you to ask God to teach you something that you will be able to apply to your own life that day. When you approach the Bible with an expectant heart, you'll never walk away empty-handed.

An Expensive But Effective Lesson

Recently, I heard about a man who received a traffic violation at a stoplight just one block from his apartment. He was making a quick trip to a grocery store down the street, and he didn't bother to put his seat belt on. After all, he was just going down the street, he thought. Well, at the stoplight, a police officer pulled up beside him and noticed he didn't have a seat belt on, which is illegal in his state. The officer motioned for him to turn into a nearby parking lot and issued him a ticket. When he realized the fine and court costs added up to well over $100, he was really upset. It was one silly mistake and now he had to pay all that money. But you know what the result has been? He says, "Every time I get in my car now, the first thing I do is put on my seat belt. I'm not going to make that mistake again. I learned my lesson."

I don't know what kind of mistakes you have made in your life. If you're like most of us, you've made quite a few. There have probably been some big ones, and there have probably been even more small ones. Mistakes and failures are part of life. But you don't have to waste those mistakes today—you can learn from each one of them.

The fine may have been more than you wanted to pay, but you don't have to pay it again. You have an opportunity to learn from the mistakes of yesterday in order to live in victory today. Don't get stuck in the past errors you have made; move past them in faith and do as Jesus said: "Go and sin no more" (John 8:11). Have a determination to improve in order to glorify God.

God has something new waiting for you. New mind-sets, new attitudes, new victories, and new opportunities. In order to enjoy the life Jesus came to give you, choose to learn from your mistakes rather than repeat them. They can serve as valuable reminders of what God has taught you along the way. I understand that mistakes are somewhat like eating vegetables and may not be your favorite part of the meal, but they're good for you. Don't waste them.

Summary:

- What some might see as failures, others see as lessons.
- The Holy Spirit brings conviction, never condemnation.
- You can learn from the mistakes of others as well as your own.
- The Bible shows us a perfect God who loves imperfect people.
- God is bringing you into something new. Don't waste the lessons you've learned along the way.

"Failure is the opportunity to begin again more intelligently."

—Henry Ford

"Keep on beginning and failing. Each time you fail, start all over again, and you will grow stronger until you have accomplished a purpose—not the one you began with, perhaps, but one you'll be glad to remember."

—Anne Sullivan
(instructor and companion of Helen Keller)

"I've failed over and over and over again in life and that is why I succeed."

—Michael Jordan

"Success is not final, failure is not fatal: it is the courage to continue that counts."

—Winston Churchill

CHAPTER 14

When All Things Become New

"Vitality shows in not only the ability to persist but the ability to start over."

—F. Scott Fitzgerald

There is something special about new beginnings. A new year, a new job, a new opportunity, a new season—I'm sure you've experienced it; there is a sense of hope that comes with a fresh start. Ed Ryder knows exactly how this feels. In fact, he knows this better than most.

In 1973, Ed Ryder was sentenced to life in prison for a murder he didn't commit. Like the plot of a legal thriller, Ryder was wrongly accused and poorly defended. There was nothing he could do but watch as his life was unjustly taken away. He spent two decades behind bars in Pennsylvania's Graterford Prison before new evidence finally cleared him of any wrongdoing. In September 1993, Governor Mark Singel commuted Ryder's sentence. Ed Ryder was 43 years old.

Upon his release, Ed found himself reborn into an everyday life most people take for granted. He said, "It seemed like...I don't know...like the oxygen was even different. You know what I mean? The air seemed to be thinner."

When asked about what he enjoyed most about his new freedom, he said he enjoyed the simplicity of choosing and making his own breakfast. "I'll tell you what's been a real kick for me: getting up and cooking breakfast; making pancakes and eggs and bacon and stuff like that. It sounds drab, but to me, that's really exciting, and that's one of the things I always dreamed of doing."

Along with the little things in life that are easy to overlook, Ed also dreamed of starting his own jazz band. While in prison, he met other musicians through the prison's artist-in-residence program. Ed played music every chance he got. Through nearly compulsive practice, Ed further developed his already impressive gift for the trumpet.

Now, upon his release, he plays his instrument, but he says he plays differently now. He said, "The first time I played when I got out of prison, I didn't feel compelled to play so exact like I did when I was at Graterford. Inmates are the most critical people in the world—they criticize anything you do. They'll find something you didn't do right."

Because of the fascinating nature of his story, people regularly ask him about his past years in prison, but Ed doesn't like to talk about the past. He points out that in prison, people don't look at the past; it's too painful. He said that in prison, the only hope was in looking to the future—to the day of your release. "When I was in prison, I dreamed about the future. I had a lot of plans. You're constantly hoping for the future."

Ed says that he still plays the same music that he did when he was in prison, but the songs mean something different to him today. He said, "I'm not in prison anymore. That's not my struggle anymore... now I hear things differently."

The Day Of Your Release

I can't imagine the difficulty that Ed Ryder endured, but I can and do admire his attitude. In the articles I read about him, he wasn't bitter or angry over his past imprisonment; instead, he was excited about his future. I couldn't help noticing the way he kept talking about how things were different now, even the way he played his music. His release changed everything—he had a brand-new life to live.

This reminds me of our lives in God. Our banner verse for this book (2 Corinthians 5:17) says that in Christ, not only is the old gone, but "the fresh and new has come!" This means we don't have to live imprisoned in the same old mindsets, fears, temptations, worries, and attitudes of the past. You've been released from those things that have kept you from enjoying your life in God. It's time to experience the new things Jesus came to give you.

> You've been released from those things that have kept you from enjoying your life in God. It's time to experience the new things Jesus came to give you.

Think about the disciples and their responses when Jesus first called each of them to follow Him. They had a choice to make: they could stay in their old lives or they could leave the old ways behind and follow Jesus into something new. Peter and Andrew didn't hesitate to make their choices in Matthew 4:18–20:

> As He was walking by the Sea of Galilee, He noticed two brothers, Simon who is called Peter and Andrew his brother, throwing a dragnet into the sea, for they were fishermen.
>
> And He said to them, Come after Me [as disciples—letting Me be your Guide], follow Me, and I will make you fishers of men!
>
> At once they left their nets and became His disciples [sided with His party and followed Him].

For Peter and Andrew, the decision was easy: they left their nets behind to follow Jesus. They exchanged the old for the new, not trying to bring their old lifestyle into their new calling.

In the same way that Jesus called Peter and Andrew to leave the old life behind and follow Him into something new—something better—He calls you to do the same. The life He has for you is one of promise and victory full of new things in God, but in order to realize the full potential of that, there will be some things that God will instruct you to walk away from. These are things that you may have grown accustomed to—bad habits, negative thinking, worry, fear, wrong confessions, etc.—but they are things that have imprisoned you. You probably won't immediately eliminate all of these bad behaviors from your life, but God will lead you daily, step by step, and you will find that as you follow Him you will always be making progress. God has something better for you. He has new things for you to embrace. Today is the day of your release.

New Attitudes

If there is no noticeable difference between the attitude of a believer and the attitude of a nonbeliever, something is wrong. We are called to be the light of the world (Matthew 5:14). And to be the light of the world, something has to be different about us—I believe that difference begins with our attitudes. The kind of attitudes we have toward God, the past, the future, ourselves, our lives, and the people around us are vital.

If you have a negative, grumpy, complaining attitude, no one is going to come up to you and say, "Wow! Something is different about you. Tell me what you have, because I really need that!" Those kinds of attitudes don't draw people to Christ. People are already negative and grumpy and complaining; they don't want more of that. You can put Christian bumper stickers on your car and Christian jewelry around your neck, but if your attitude is bad, people won't see Jesus.

A bad attitude will also affect you. If you are living your life with defeated thinking and a discouraged mind-set, you are missing out

> *If you are living your life with defeated thinking and a discouraged mind-set, you are missing out on the joyful, overcoming life Jesus came to give you.*

on the joyful, overcoming life Jesus came to give you. He doesn't want you to go through each day angry or frustrated; He wants you to go through life happy and confident, knowing that God has a great plan for your life.

I used to have a very negative attitude. I loved God and I wanted to be happy, but I rarely had a positive attitude. For many years in my life, this was an area of struggle for me. One of the things God showed me is that attitude is a result of perspective. How I chose to view a situation determined how I responded to it.

For example, if Dave would go play golf instead of spending the morning with me, I would get so upset. My perspective would be, "How could he leave me by myself this morning?! Doesn't he know I wanted to spend time with him?" But when God began to change my perspective, my attitude began to change. Instead of getting angry with Dave, I chose to focus on how thankful I was for Dave. Instead of thinking about what I couldn't do when he was out, I chose to focus on the things I'd be able to get done during those few hours. Now, when Dave wants to go play golf, I think, "Okay, that will give me time to get some work done...or be alone and enjoy the total quiet in the house...or maybe go shopping!"

That's just one example, but I want you to see that what you choose to focus on can really affect your attitude. If you focus on your problems or your frustrations, your attitude is going to be negative and defeated. But when you put your focus on God and His promises for your life, your attitude will immediately change. That's

> *When you put your focus on God and His promises for your life, your attitude will immediately change.*

why David said, "I lift up my eyes to the mountains—where does my help come from? My help comes from the Lord, the Maker of heaven and earth" (Psalm 121:1–2 NIV). David knew that his spirit would be affected by his perspective and focus. When trouble came, David looked up—he looked to the Lord instead of looking at his problems.

Your attitude belongs to you, and nobody can force you to have a bad one if you refuse to do so. Viktor Frank spent several years in a concentration camp during the Holocaust. There were many things taken away from him that he could do nothing about, but he determined to keep a good attitude, saying that was something no one could take away from him.

The inconveniences, frustrations, and anxieties of life that used to drag you down are nothing compared to the promises of God in your life. You have something to be excited about today. God is for you, and He is working on your behalf. Cheer up and be encouraged—it's all going to work out. One of my favorite verses says:

> *We are assured and know that [God being a partner in their labor] all things work together and are [fitting into a plan] for good to and for those who love God and are called according to [His] design and purpose.* (Romans 8:28)

That's an attitude-changer! You can go through each day with a happy realization that God is working all things for your good. He loves you, and He has a great plan for your life. Let that be your focus, and let your light shine for all to see.

New Confessions

If you are looking for God to do something new in your life today, I want to encourage you to begin making new confessions. The words you say are setting the course for your life. The words you speak have the power to affect your joy, your prayers, and your future.

Have you ever been around someone who always sees the negative in a situation? They seem to constantly be talking about how terrible everything is, how tough they've got it, or how mad they are. I've known people like this (and I used to be this way myself). When they're starting to feel better, they say, "I'm still a little sick!" When the weather is clearing up, they say, "It's still cloudy!" These are people who see the worst—and *say* the worst.

If you've noticed, people who live like that are never happy. I know I sure wasn't. Before I learned about the power of my words, I was miserable because I was speaking fear, speaking dysfunction, speaking death over my life. As long as you rehearse your problems and speak your fears, you are going to live captive to problems and fears. But it's not too late to make new confessions. Positive, faith-filled words will undo the results of the negative, murmuring, complaining, and fearful ones we have spoken in the past.

> *The moment you begin to confess God's Word over your life and get in agreement with God by speaking faith into your situation, things begin to change.*

The moment you begin to confess God's Word over your life and get in agreement with God by speaking faith into your situation, things begin to change.

- Instead of speaking, "I'm never going to get better," confess, "I am healed by the stripes of Jesus!" (Isaiah 53:5) Expect improvement daily!
- Instead of speaking, "There is just no way I can make it through this situation," confess, "God is making a way where there seems to be no way!" (Isaiah 40:4)
- Instead of speaking, "There is no way I can accomplish that," confess, "I can do all things through Christ Jesus!" (Philippians 4:13)

- Instead of speaking, "I'm not talented enough," confess, "I am created in the image of God; I am fearfully and wonderfully made." (Psalm 139:14)

As a believer, it's time to make some new confessions. When you confess God's promises over your circumstance, you speak life to your spirit and things begin to change. Don't give strength to negative thoughts or defeated thinking; choose to speak God's Word over your life and see what a difference it will make.

New Rest

I meet people all the time who are tired...actually, they're exhausted. Their schedules have become so hectic, and the cares of their lives have become so heavy, that they are living burned-out, stressed-out lives.

It you can relate to that, I want you to know that God has something new for you today—something better. Jesus came to give you a life full of peace and rest, a life full of joy in the Lord. Tired, run-down, worn-out lives are the old way of things. You don't have to live in that prison anymore; Jesus came to set you free. I love what the author of Hebrews says about God's rest:

> *Therefore, while the promise of entering His rest still holds and is offered [today], let us be afraid [to distrust it], lest any of you should think he has come too late and has come short of [reaching] it. (Hebrews 4:1)*

What an amazing passage of Scripture. Rest isn't wishful thinking—rest is the "promise" of God for your life. And you are not "too late" to receive it. It is never too late to learn to live peacefully! Whatever stresses or pressures you are going through today, you

> *Rest isn't wishful thinking—rest is the "promise" of God for your life.*

can cast those cares on the Lord (1 Peter 5:7) and receive His rest. You can enjoy your life because God loves you unconditionally and He cares for you.

I've noticed I leave God's rest when I think it's my job to fix the problem or figure out a solution; however, when I realize that God can handle this situation better than I ever could and turn it over to Him, I return to that place of rest. It doesn't mean that I never plan or problem-solve, but it means that I ask God for His wisdom and simply trust Him with the results. I believe the same will be true for you. If you will choose to let go of the pressure of having to be the person to fix everything and trust that God will have His way in your life, you will find a new level of rest that you have never experienced before.

Ask yourself this question: "What do I spend more time doing... worrying or worshipping?" If the answer is worrying, leave those nets—that old lifestyle—behind and bring every worrisome situation to the Lord in prayer and worship Him. That is the key to rest. That is the key to a new beginning.

A Wisdom Story

I came across a short modern-day parable that I want to share with you:

> There once was a woman who woke up one morning, looked in the mirror, and noticed she had only three hairs on her head. "Well," she said, "I think I'll braid my hair today." So she did and she had a wonderful day.
>
> The next day she woke up, looked in the mirror, and saw that she had only two hairs on her head. "Hmmm," she said,

"I think I'll part my hair down the middle today." So she did and she had a grand day.

The next day she woke up, looked in the mirror, and noticed that she had only one hair on her head. "Well," she said, "Today I'm going to wear my hair in a ponytail." So she did, and she had a fun, fun day.

The next day she woke up, looked in the mirror, and noticed that there wasn't a single hair on her head. "YAY!" she exclaimed. "I don't have to fix my hair today!"

This is a woman who understood the power of a good attitude. Her attitude, her confession, and her choice to rest allowed her to see life differently. They allowed her to enjoy her life regardless of the situation she faced.

I don't know what circumstances you face today, but I want you to know that a new beginning awaits you. And God allows you to play a vital role in that new beginning. Your attitude, your confessions, and your choice to rest will greatly affect your life, today and each day moving forward.

Like the disciples, like Ed Ryder, and like the woman in our parable, the choice is yours. You can decide to live in the old mind-sets, attitudes, temptations, fears, and worries that used to imprison you, or you can live in the new thing God has for you. Though you may be accustomed to the old way, the new beginning is better. Sure, the music may sound different, the air might feel thinner, but you'll never want to go back ever again.

Summary:

- When you are in Christ, all things become new.
- Your perspective determines your attitude. What are you focusing on: your problems or your promises from God?

- The words you say will set the course of your life. This is why it is important to speak God's Word over your situation.
- It's not too late to enter God's rest. You don't have to live a stressed-out life.
- You have been released from the past. You can live in the new things God has for you today.

Praise be to the God and Father of our Lord Jesus Christ! In his great mercy he has given us new birth into a living hope through the resurrection of Jesus Christ from the dead.

1 Peter 1:3 (NIV)

CHAPTER 15

Plan B: B Stands For Better

"What we obtain too cheap, we esteem too lightly."

—Thomas Paine

Sometimes *Plan A* doesn't work out. Have you noticed that to be true? Whether it's a little plan or a big plan, your daily schedule or your career strategy, plans have a way of disappointing us. *The dinner is burned. The job is boring. The book doesn't get published. The outfit is too small. The contract ends. The spouse leaves. The flight is canceled.* See what I mean? Sometimes *Plan A* is a bust. It is disappointing to have our own plans fail, but if we feel that we have messed up God's *Plan A* for our lives, it is easy to slip into despair and feel hopeless.

Many people fall apart when their plan falls apart. (I used to be one of them.) And it doesn't even have to be over anything major. If the wait at the restaurant is longer than promised...dinner is ruined. If their favorite show fails to record one evening...meltdown. Even small disappointments turn into significant devastations. (If you've ever pulled up to a Chick-fil-A drive-thru on a Sunday, you know exactly what I'm talking about—"But I had my heart set on WAFFLE FRIES!!!" I do, however, respect them for closing on Sunday to honor God and give everyone a day of rest.)

More seriously, it's the big disappointments that do the most damage. I meet people all the time who think it's too late to enjoy their lives because *Plan A* crumbled. *He didn't propose. The bank foreclosed.*

Their marriage failed. The family business went belly-up. They haven't gotten pregnant. The stock market crashed. They didn't get the job. The really sad part is that some of these people are still reeling from a failed plan that occurred many years ago. I'm sure you know what I'm talking about; you probably know someone who is still stuck in a distant disappointment. (You may be stuck there yourself.)

Well, I have good news for anyone disappointed or disillusioned by his or her original plan. I've discovered that *Plan B* is often better than *Plan A* ever could have been. I may not have realized that truth in the midst of *Plan A* unraveling, but when I looked back on it—weeks, months, or even years later—I couldn't believe how much better the situation turned out to be. As a matter of fact, there have been many times when I got on my knees and thanked God that He didn't let *Plan A* work out. I was so much happier because *Plan B* was so much better.

That's why I think it's important to remember that sometimes *B stands for better.*

Harrison knows what I'm talking about—he experienced this firsthand...

When Failure Sets You Up For Success

Harrison moved to California with high hopes. High hopes that faded pretty quickly. Originally, he thought he would be able to do voice-over work, but that didn't pan out. He even tried to make a living doing bit parts in Hollywood movies, but that never paid the bills. Disappointed and low on cash, Harrison needed to figure out a way to support his wife and two children, so he came up with his own plan: he would build things. He knew his way around a hammer and power saw, so he decided to take up carpentry as his chosen profession. It wasn't a particularly exciting idea, but it was the best idea he had. *Plan A* was under way.

Harrison had no official carpentry experience, but he threw himself into his new endeavor, reading carpentry books and learning by trial and error. He started by building a pair of tables for a friend. This led to other small jobs that he was contracted to do. Good word of mouth kept him busy. Eventually, he was taking on significant projects like building recording studios for well-known composers. Whatever it was—big or small—if you needed it built, Harrison was your man.

One day, while he was installing a door on a Hollywood movie set, a relatively unknown movie director named George Lucas asked Harrison to put down the hammer for a few minutes and help him with some auditions. Lucas wanted the carpenter to read with the potential actors who were trying out for an upcoming science-fiction movie. After Harrison spent the afternoon reading with some very famous actors, Lucas stopped the auditions—he had found his man in the carpenter.

George Lucas was so impressed with Harrison's talent and natural charisma, he decided to offer the carpenter a role in his movie. Harrison Ford went on to star as Han Solo in George Lucas's *Star Wars*. The science-fiction thriller is still considered one of the most successful film trilogies of all time, and Harrison Ford is a household name who has made millions of dollars as a Hollywood leading man.

Plan A was fine. *Plan B* was better.

Hold On To Your Plan Loosely

Harrison Ford's story teaches us a simple but valuable lesson: hold on to your plans loosely—there may be a better plan ahead. This is especially true in the life of a believer. As children of God, we know that God has a plan for our lives. Jeremiah 29:11 is a very familiar passage of Scripture that speaks about the plan God has in store for you, a plan that will "prosper" you and give you "hope and a future."

"For I know the plans I have for you," declares the Lord, "plans to prosper you and not to harm you, plans to give you hope and a future." (Jeremiah 29:11 NIV)

Before you read another page of this book, I want you to really understand that God has a great plan for your life, a plan that will bring the peace and joy that Jesus came to give you. If you've surrendered your life to Him and submitted to His guidance, you don't have to fear when any plan disappoints. You know that God has you in the palm of His hand. Instead of living in fear and worry because *Plan A* fell apart, I want you to look at it through the eyes of faith.

> *God has a great plan for your life, a plan that will bring the peace and joy that Jesus came to give you.*

Here is what I mean: If *Plan A* isn't working out, understand that God is doing something better. You may not understand what it is at the time, but this is where faith comes in. I've found that when our plans fall apart, God may be doing one of these four things:

1. Protecting You From Something

Anytime you talk about plans, you have to begin by asking, "Whose plan is this anyway? Is this my plan or is this God's plan?" I say that because the only way you are going to really enjoy your life is if you pursue the plan God has for you. His plan is always best. Sadly, we often forget that. Sometimes we get so impressed by the plans *we've* made for our lives that we never stop and ask God what *He* has planned.

In our zeal to accomplish our goals, it's easy to run with the wrong plan. It doesn't mean that you have bad motives or are purposely trying to do the wrong thing; it just means that you still haven't heard God clearly. I'm not saying that you should never make plans;

however, when you do make plans and set goals for your life, always remember to submit those to the Lord. I think it's wise to go to God and say, "Lord, this is what I'm thinking You want me to do in this situation, or this is what I think You want me to do in my life, but if this isn't Your plan, I trust You to point me in the right direction." And then trust God as you walk that decision out. If it is not His plan for your life, the Lord will show you.

People think that God leads us by opening doors of opportunity (and that's true—He often does that), but they don't realize that He can lead you just as easily by closing doors. If you're living for God and trusting His guidance for your life and the plan falls apart, God may be protecting you from something.

> *If you're living for God and trusting His guidance for your life and the plan falls apart, God may be protecting you from something.*

If you tried your best to restore a friendship, but that friend insisted on ending the relationship, God may be leading by closing a door. That may have been a friendship that would cause you damage down the road.

If you did the work required and tried to get into a certain college, but they rejected your application, God may be protecting you from an event that would harm you.

If you worked as hard as you could, but your employer laid you off, God may be protecting you from a career that would never fulfill you or provide enough for your family.

Just because something doesn't work out doesn't mean you failed. It may mean that God is protecting you and guiding you away from what was *your* plan in order to guide you into *His* plan.

This leads us to the next thing God is often doing when the plan seems to be going haywire...

2. Producing Something In You

When I read the Gospels, I often chuckle at Peter's mishaps. It seems that he is always getting into some kind of trouble. His plans rarely work out the way he thinks they will. Look at these examples:

> When Jesus told the disciples that He was going to Jerusalem to die, Peter pulled Jesus aside privately, telling Him that this must never happen. Jesus responded by saying, "Get behind me, Satan" (Matthew 16:23 NIV). *Yikes! Unsuccessful plan.* Just imagine how embarrassed Peter must have been!
>
> When he saw Jesus walking on the water, Peter wanted to walk on the water with the Lord. (At least he had the courage to get out of the boat!) He took a few successful steps, but when he felt the wind and looked at the waves, Peter began to sink (Matthew 14). *Help! Not a totally successful plan.*
>
> When he was confronted with a mob of soldiers who intended to take Jesus away, Peter planned to fight them off. When he pulled out his sword and cut off the soldier's ear, Jesus rebuked him and healed the soldier he wounded (John 18). *Oops! Unsuccessful plan.*

But in every failed plan Peter endured, Jesus used it to teach him—Jesus was producing character in Peter that would enable him to fulfill his destiny. The Bible shows us that Peter would go on to preach on the Day of Pentecost and throughout his entire life, and help establish the early church. You or I might think, "Why choose Peter for these tasks? Peter kept failing." But with each failed plan, God was producing something in Peter's heart. Even when *Plan A* fails, because God is so amazing, He can make *Plan B* better than *Plan A* ever could have been!

There is a lot to be learned when you go through a trial. If you think about it, probably some of the biggest things you've learned

If you think about it, probably some of the biggest things you've learned in life were taught through difficult situations.

in life were taught through difficult situations. The situation was not easy and you wouldn't want to go through it again, but it taught you a lot about God's faithfulness and mercy, and a lot about yourself.

That's why I tell people all the time, "Don't waste your trials, your failure, or your mistakes." There are so many things to be learned when you go through hard times because it is in these times that you are leaning on the Lord. In times of trial, God can do a deep work in your heart because of your dependence on Him. Romans chapter 5 says it this way:

> . . . *Let us exult and triumph in our troubles and rejoice in our sufferings, knowing that pressure and affliction and hardship produce patient and unswerving endurance.*
>
> *And endurance (fortitude) develops maturity of character (approved faith and tried integrity). And character [of this sort] produces [the habit of] joyful and confident hope of eternal salvation. (Romans 5:3–4)*

I know it sounds counterintuitive to actually "exult and triumph" or "rejoice" when you are struck with disappointment, and if you aren't trusting God, it probably sounds a little bit crazy. But when you know that God is with you and you choose to stand in faith knowing that He has a great plan for your life, you know that He can use a broken plan to produce something beautiful.

God wasn't surprised when *Plan A* failed. He exists outside of time, and He knows the end from the beginning. He can use any situation to produce something good in your life. When you go through something difficult, instead of spending your entire prayer time asking God to deliver you from it, I encourage you to stop and ask God to do something amazing in the midst of it. Pray: "God, what is

it that You are trying to develop in my life through this situation?"
You might be surprised to find that He is using the very difficulty
you are trying to avoid to prepare you for something important
in your life.

That brings us to one more thing that God may be doing when
Plan A doesn't work out...

3. Preparing You For Something Greater

I can look back on my life and see that many of the things God
began (and ended) in my life were in order to prepare me for something greater. God never takes us backward—He always takes us
forward into greater things with Him. We may not understand what
He is doing at the time, but that doesn't change the fact that He is
doing something amazing in our lives. Isaiah 55:9 tells us:

> *For as the heavens are higher than the earth, so are My
> ways higher than your ways and My thoughts than your
> thoughts.*

That means God has a game plan for our lives that is greater than
what we can comprehend. If we will trust Him to execute His plan,
He will do everything that needs to be done in order to bring us into
what He has prepared.

I think about my kids when they were just toddlers. The first time
I took them to the park, they had no idea what was awaiting them. I
knew how much they would love the sandboxes, swing sets, jungle
gym, and every climbing contraption a little kid could imagine, but
before we went, I had to prepare them. I had to take them away from
the little, plastic play set at home, put them in the car, and drive
them to the park. You would have thought I was the worst parent
ever! They cried and cried, just so upset that they had to stop playing and get in the car. *How could I ruin their day like that?* But when

they saw where I was taking them, their entire disposition changed. They no longer cared about the small, plastic play set at home—this park was the coolest thing they had ever seen!

Here is what I want you to see: If your plan isn't working out, be open to the fact that God will use it to prepare you for something better. That relationship, that career, that opportunity called *Plan A*, even though it failed, may be what He uses to get you into position for a better plan. The plan that seems to have fallen apart may be the little, plastic play set you're driving away from on your way to the jungle gym you'll never want to leave!

4. Teaching You That All Things Really Are Possible With God

Your plan may have failed because it was never God's plan to begin with, but even if *Plan A* was God's original plan and you messed it up completely, it is still not too late for you to have a great life. As I said earlier, with God, *Plan B* can be better than *Plan A* ever could have been. We may not understand it, but with God all things are possible. God is truly AMAZING!!!

God forgives and forgets our past sins and mistakes and treats us as if they never happened. Even though there may be some lingering consequences from our failures, in God they can be dealt with and overcome. God created everything we see in nature out of nothing, so surely He can do something with our mistakes and failures. Even a failure is more than nothing. It may not be anything good, but it is something. And when we give what we have to God, even if it is our failures, His creative powers go to work, turning it into something wonderful and amazing.

> God forgives and forgets our past sins and mistakes and treats us as if they never happened.

Joseph Had A Plan

In Genesis chapter 37, Joseph had a dream of greatness. He told his family all about it (even though it involved ruling over them) and almost gloated about his potential. *Plan A* was looking great. If he was anything like you or me, I'm sure he was planning all the ways his life might go in order for him to be a success. But his plans fell apart quickly.

If you are familiar with the Bible, you know how the story goes. Joseph was kidnapped by his older brothers and sold into slavery. After serving for years as a slave in Egypt, he was falsely accused by Potiphar's wife and thrown in prison. He spent many years in prison, and just when it looked like he might be freed, he was forgotten. *Broken plans, crumbled dreams, deep disappointment.*

If that were the end of Joseph's story, what a sad story it would be. But God wasn't done with Joseph's life. Through a series of miraculous events, Joseph was freed from prison, brought before Pharaoh, and promoted to the second highest position in the government. He would also be the instrument that God would use to save his family and his people from a seven-year famine.

At the end of the story, when Joseph is reunited with his family, he tells his brothers, "You intended to harm me, but God intended it for good to accomplish what is now being done, the saving of many lives" (Genesis 50:20 NIV). Joseph could look back and see that God was working behind the scenes for something better the whole time. Every step of the way, God used the seemingly bad to protect him, produce something in him, prepare him for something greater, and teach him all things are possible. God took the bad and turned it into something good!

The same is true in your life. God is using every situation for your good. His plan is not a secondary plan—it's not a fallback plan. God's plan for your life is the plan that should always be considered *The New Plan A*. If something you planned doesn't work or if a door seems to close, don't assume you'll have to settle for something less; believe that you're going to see something greater.

If other people want to call that *Plan B*, that's okay, don't try to stop them. You and I both know ... *B stands for better.*

Summary:

- God's plan for your life is greater than any plan you could come up with on your own.
- Submit your plans to God and ask Him for wisdom and guidance.
- If a plan doesn't work out, God may be protecting you from something that would hurt you.
- God can use even difficult things to produce godly character in your heart.
- Trust that the Lord is preparing you for something even greater.
- God is teaching you that all things are possible with Him.

Previous Tweets From @joycemeyer: God's Plan Is Always Better (Feel free to share.)

God is working in you and in your life right now. You may not feel it or see it, but you can believe it!

Faith means that you have peace even when you don't have all the answers.

If you believe God loves you, has a plan for your life, and that His timing is always right, there is no need to envy anyone.

Practice being positive in every situation. God has promised to bring good out of whatever is taking place in your life at the moment.

Being positive does not mean we deny the existence of difficulty; it means we believe God is greater than our difficulties.

Patience is not the ability to wait, but how you act while you're waiting.

Instead of worrying about your problems, worship, sing, praise, and give thanks to God. Then watch and see what happens in your life.

We are more than conquerors through Christ! Before you ever have a problem, He has the answer.

The best thing about your attitude is that it's yours, and you can choose to change it!

We will fail in life, but that doesn't mean that you are a failure.

God can take "Plan B" and make it better than "Plan A" ever would have been.

We're never without a way because Jesus is The Way.

You're never too old, or too young, to do something amazing with God.

When we fall down, God is always there to pick us back up.

CHAPTER 16

A New Dream

"You are never too old to set another goal or dream a new dream."

—C. S. Lewis

The longer you are a Christian and the more time you spend in the Word, the easier it is to gloss over familiar passages of Scripture. In our Bible reading time, we're tempted to think, "Oh, I've read this story before," and then just skim over the words, ready to check off a box on our spiritual disciplines list. This is why I always encourage people to do more than just *read* the Word—*study* it. If you approach the Bible each day with an expectant heart, prepared to slow down, and really meditate on what the Lord is saying, you'll get so much more out of your time with God.

I think the story of Moses is a perfect example.

When I mention Moses, you probably picture him in Pharaoh's court, thundering boldly, "Let my people go!" Or maybe you see him in front of the Red Sea with his outreached staff causing the waters to part and the people to marvel. You may even think of him walking up the mountain to receive the Ten Commandments from God Himself. These images are reinforced regularly through the pictures, movies, stories, and sermons we view and hear on a frequent basis. I had someone on my staff look up "Moses" on *Google*

Images, and there are hundreds of pictures displaying an impressive, self-assured, confident portrait of this man.

Now, there is nothing wrong with those pictures of Moses. He *was* a powerful leader, used mightily by God. But I'd like to remind you that the Bible tells us a lot more about the life of Moses—Moses wasn't always challenging pharaohs and parting seas. When we happen upon Moses at the beginning of Exodus chapter 3, Moses was just a shepherd. And he's not a young shepherd, either (like David was in the book of First Samuel)—Moses was 80 years old, watching sheep for his father-in-law. Hardly the image of a successful leader.

By this point in his life, Moses was an experienced shepherd too. He had tended sheep on the back side of the Midian wilderness for 40 long years (Exodus 3:1; Acts 7:30). Instead of rushing through the text, let's think about that for a minute. *Four decades of long, lonely days with nothing to do except think of what might have been. Four decades of wondering if he should have done things differently. Four decades of watching his dream slip away.*

Earlier in Exodus, we read that Moses was raised in the house of Pharaoh. Though he was a Hebrew baby, he was raised as a prince. (Pharaoh's daughter rescued him from genocide and concealed his Hebrew heritage from the public.) Moses lived the first 40 years of his life in Pharaoh's palace (Acts 7:23). I wonder how many times he dreamed of delivering his people from Egyptian oppression. The Bible says that it was in his heart "to help them and to care for them" (Acts 7:23). In fact, he was so anxious to be a deliverer, he tried to do it in his own strength, killing an Egyptian who was beating a Hebrew slave (Exodus 2:12).

This act of violence was his undoing. He was forced to flee Egypt as a fugitive, living in hiding as a shepherd in Midian. This is where we find him at the beginning of chapter 3. He spent 40 years waiting to be a deliverer—now 40 years waiting to be delivered from the mess he'd gotten himself into. These last 40 years were spent doing nothing particularly important, working for someone else, and possibly feeling a bit disappointed about how his life had turned out.

> *One of the great things about the Bible is we see God using normal, flawed people.*

One of the great things about the Bible is we see God using normal, flawed people. Moses is more than a Sunday school legend. He's a regular person who probably felt like he blew his best chance. In the years he spent leading sheep instead of leading people, I wonder how many times Moses assumed the dream was dead; how many times he thought he was too old to do anything important; how many times he regretted his past or dreaded his future.

We don't know what went through his mind during those years in the wilderness, but we do know that he was surprised when God spoke to him from the burning bush. His first response was, "Who am I, that I should go..." (Exodus 3:11). Basically, he was saying, "Lord, You must be looking for somebody else." Whether he thought he was too old, too flawed, too inadequate, or just too late, he was surprised by this new chance.

You probably know the rest of the story—God wouldn't take "no" for an answer. He answered Moses' question of "Who am I?" with His promise, "I AM WHO I AM" (Exodus 3:14), and He sent Moses back to Egypt to deliver the people. Moses became the biblical hero we know him to be because God showed up in the wilderness and gave him a fresh start—a new beginning. After seemingly hearing from the Lord, for the first time in 40 years, Moses was able to dream again.

It's Never Too Late To Dream Again

No book about new beginnings with God would be complete if it didn't talk about a new dream. I believe that every person should have a dream for their life and then go after that dream with all their heart. In the previous chapter, we talked about the plans in your life, but this is different. Plans are manageable opportunities, but dreams are often too big to be managed. You plan to assemble a model airplane…you dream to fly.

Dreams always require faith because they are bigger than you or your ability to accomplish them. That is why I believe faith-filled dreams are so important—"Without faith it is impossible to please God" (Hebrews 11:6 NIV). When you dream a big dream for God, you become totally dependent on Him. You seek Him more, you trust Him more, and you recognize your need for Him because you know you can't do it on your own.

> Dreams always require faith because they are bigger than you or your ability to accomplish them.

Every dreamer comes to the point where they stop and say, "Lord, this is the dream I believe You've given me, but I don't know how to make it happen. I need You to make this dream come true. I need You to lead the way." This is a beautiful prayer. It's a prayer that is less about self and more about God.

In the story of Moses, God reminds us it's never too late to dream again. At one point in his life, Moses may have looked like the person to do great things for God, but not now. In the natural, it looked like he was finished: *He had messed up. He was too old. No one even knew where he was.* But God knew where Moses was, and He wasn't finished with him yet.

Maybe you can relate to that today. Maybe you can understand Moses' situation better than most. If you've gone through a personal failure, found yourself living below your potential, or feel like you're still hidden in a wilderness, be encouraged; none of that can stop the work of the Holy Spirit in your life. God can show up and ignite any dream if you will believe.

- It's not too late to dream about ministering the Word.
- It's not too late to dream about owning your own business.
- It's not too late to dream about being debt-free.

- It's not too late to dream about having that family.
- It's not too late to dream about reaching that goal.
- It's not too late to dream for your children to do great things for God.
- It's not too late to dream a relationship will be restored.
- It's not too late to dream that all the wasted years of your life can be redeemed, and that *Plan B* can be better than *Plan A* ever could have been.

It's important to point out that I'm not talking about daydreaming. As Christians, we aren't called to sit around and do nothing, wishing for better things. When God puts a dream in your heart, He will show you the steps to take to participate as He makes that dream a reality. Always remember that faith is active, not passive. In 1 Corinthians 15:10, Paul said, "I worked harder than all of them . . ." (his part), but everything Paul did was in obedience and through the power of the Lord (God's part). Paul was willing to work, and God gave him grace to do it.

When God spoke to Moses about being a part of something bigger than himself (delivering the Hebrew people from Egyptian oppression), Moses didn't just sit around thinking, "Wow! God gave me a dream of what He wants to do with my life. One day it might come true." He made his faith active, taking steps to fulfill the plan of God. God was faithful to show him what to do and give him the strength to do it, but Moses still took the opportunity to step out in faith and *do* something.

> When God puts a dream in your heart, He will show you the steps to take to participate as He makes that dream a reality.

If you ask God to give you a new dream, I believe He will.

> If you ask God to give you a new dream, I believe He will.

If you don't feel that God has given you a dream, then reconnect with what is in your heart. Ask yourself what you love to do and enjoy the most. What are you good at? God leads us in many different ways and it is often in very normal ways. When we speak of hearing from God, it doesn't mean you should listen for a booming voice from Heaven, or watch for an angel to appear with a message. Following your heart is the best way to begin. God won't have you spend your life doing something that you hate and are really lousy at.

The Word of God says He will "do superabundantly, far over and above all that we [dare] ask or think [infinitely beyond our highest prayers, desires, thoughts, hopes, or dreams]" (Ephesians 3:20). That passage is full of dream words: "superabundantly," "far over," and "infinitely beyond." God wants to do something great in your life!!

Doing The Impossible

As you read the Bible, you see God calling improbable people to do impossible things. Time and time again, we read about people who thought they had missed their chance, but God did something amazing: He gave them a new dream.

Esther was taken as a concubine for King Xerxes. She would eventually become queen, and God would use her to save the Israelites from destruction. One woman saved a nation.

Abraham and Sarah couldn't have children. Sarah was barren, and they were both too old. But God spoke to them and told them they would have a son, and through their lineage, the world would be saved.

Peter denied he even knew the Lord. When the pressure got too great and the accusations started flying, Peter let himself down. He thought it was all over now. But God restored Peter and empowered him to preach mightily.

Saul was a Pharisee and a persecutor of the Church. He seemed like the last person God would use. But many times the last person we think God will use is the first person He chooses. On the Road to Damascus, Saul became Paul, and he went on to write two-thirds of the New Testament.

Still Dreaming

Thirty-seven years ago, God gave me a dream to teach His Word. At the time, I didn't know where that dream would take me, but I believed God was leading. I had a burning desire to share the truth of God's Word with people who were hurting—physically, emotionally, and spiritually. God brought me through so much in my life that I passionately wanted to share what He was teaching me with others around the world.

I'm amazed at what God allows me to be a part of. By His grace, I've led conferences, written books, broadcast television shows, and a whole lot more. Like those flawed characters in the Bible, God has used my life to help others in spite of my imperfections. As I look back on all that God has done, I imagine

> *God keeps giving me new dreams!*

some people might start winding down about this time. They might assume the dream is fulfilled and it is time to retire. But God keeps giving me new dreams! I may be older in years, but He keeps renewing me inwardly day by day.

For example, one of those dreams is our missions outreach, *Hand of Hope*. When we started *Hand of Hope* 25 years ago, it was in obedience to a desire that God put in my heart to help the poor. We had no idea how big it would grow or what God would do. All I knew was every time I saw hungry, homeless, sick, and lost people around the world, I wanted to help meet their needs. So we took steps to follow that dream. I'm so excited that now, years later, in addition to teaching God's Word, we help feed starving children, rescue trafficked women, dig fresh wells, care for orphans, build medical clinics, care for inner-city children, and bring aid to disaster victims all over the world. God is doing amazing things!

And you know what? I'm still dreaming. I'm dreaming that in God's strength we will continue to do more. We're not going to settle where we are; we're going to seek God for new opportunities to help those who are hurting throughout the world. I have many goals. For example, I want to see our ministries feeding one million children every single day. That's just one of the many dreams that God has placed in my heart. When I calculate what it would cost and the manpower it would take, I know that it is impossible without God, but it doesn't cost anything to dream. I want God to know that I'm available if He needs me; I am still dreaming!!! And in the meantime, we continue to increase the number of children we are feeding each year.

I share that with you for a reason. If I can keep dreaming after all these years, you can too. Wherever you are in life—young or old, hurting or healed, in the palace or in the wilderness—dream a dream. Ask God to put something in your heart so big that it can only happen by His power. And then take the steps that God shows you to take and never give up!

Summary:

- When you read the Bible, take time to study and meditate on what God is saying.
- It's never too late to dream of what God can do in your life.
- When God gives you a dream, He'll also give you the steps to take in order to see it come true.
- God uses regular people to accomplish His purposes in the world.
- Dreams are the side effects of faith.

The Power Of A Dream

It started like so many evenings. Mom and Dad at home and Jimmy playing after dinner. Mom and Dad were absorbed with jobs and did not notice the time. It was a full moon and some of the light seeped through the windows. Then Mom glanced at the clock. "Jimmy, it's time to go to bed. Go up now and I'll come and settle you later."

Unlike usual, Jimmy went straight upstairs to his room. An hour or so later his mother came up to check if all was well, and to her astonishment found that her son was staring quietly out of his window at the moonlit scenery. "What are you doing, Jimmy?" "I'm looking at the moon, Mommy." "Well, it's time to go to bed now." As the reluctant boy settled down, he said, "Mommy, you know one day I'm going to walk on the moon."

Who could have known that the boy in whom the dream was planted that night would survive a near-fatal motorbike crash that broke almost every bone in his body, and would bring to fruition this dream 32 years later when James Irwin stepped on the moon's surface, just one of the 12 representatives of the human race to have done so?

—(Author Unknown)

186

CHAPTER 17

The Greatest Story Ever Told

"There is no greater agony than bearing an untold story inside you."

—Maya Angelou

We all see the same world, but a little differently. God created each of us with unique gifts and talents, and those gifts and talents affect the way we look at the world around us. Artists see colors that you or I may have never noticed, perpetually capturing and savoring moments. Poets hear language more fluidly than most; what another person views as a conversation, they see as a dance. Mathematicians look for an underlying order and structure, leaving no room for unresolved issues over the course of any given day. Musicians move through their lives to rhythms, and if there is no obvious rhythm, they create one.

I'm a teacher by nature. I like to uncover truths and expound upon principles and precepts in order to help people and encourage them in their walk with the Lord. That's just what I love to do. I am always thinking about how to turn the things that I experience and learn into messages that will help people. I might see a statement on a billboard while driving down the highway and think, *"That would be a great title for a message about . . ."* I also love to weave God's Word into stories from real life or parables that will help people understand the Word more fully.

That's why I want to use this last chapter to tell you an amazing story. I spent hours scouring the Internet, reading books and periodicals, and even asking friends for a great story to use as a grand finale. I want you to finish the book and think, "Wow! What a great story, Joyce." "Wow! What a wonderful chapter, Joyce." "Wow! What a perfect ending to the book, Joyce." But as I searched for the perfect and most important story, I realized it's *your* story that this book is really written about. The one you are living…the one you have yet to finish…the one you will use to encourage someone else.

I don't know if you've stopped to think about this, but *your* story with God is the greatest story you know—simply because you're the one living it. You understand the highs and the lows, the wins and the losses, the laughter and the tears better than anyone else ever could. You know how far the Lord

> There is something unique and powerful about the ongoing story of your walk with God.

has brought you, and you know how far you still have to go. There is something unique and powerful about the ongoing story of your walk with God—that's why your story is the perfect story for chapter 17.

Live Your Own Story

As you live your life for God, let me remind you that you aren't called to be anyone else. Don't look at the people around you and feel that you have to compete with them, copy them, or criticize them to find happiness. If you spend your life focused on someone else's story, you're going to be a frustrated, worried, unhappy Christian. Instead of looking around at other people, look to the Lord. He is doing something unique and original in your life. When you focus on God and the work He is doing in your heart, the frustrations of comparison will melt away.

The Bible shows us that the temptation to compare yourself with someone else is nothing new. The disciples often got caught up in the same trap. In John chapter 21—after Jesus resurrected from the grave, but before His ascension into heaven—Jesus was talking to Peter about God's plan for Peter's life. Peter looks over at John and asks, "Lord, what about this man?" (v. 21). Instead of focusing on his own life, Peter was focusing on John's life. Jesus responded pretty bluntly. He said to Peter, "...What is that to you? [What concern is it of yours?] You follow Me!" (v. 22).

I think this is the same thing the Lord is saying today: "You follow Me!" Focus on following Jesus. Developing your relationship with God and obeying what He is telling you to do will keep you busy...and it will keep you happy! I encourage you not to waste your days focused on being like someone else. If you're Peter, don't try to be John. If you're Mary, don't try to be Sally. If you're Bill, don't try to be Fred. Just be the person God created you to be—you!

Many times, we compare ourselves to others because we have a negative view of ourselves. We see a gift or a talent in our coworker, our neighbor, or the lady who sings on the stage at church, and we feel we don't measure up. But let me remind you that you were created by God Himself, and when you question your worth, you're questioning God's work. Ephesians 2:10 says this about the work God did when He created you (and when He saved you):

> *When you question your worth, you're questioning God's work.*

> *For we are God's [own] handiwork (His workmanship), recreated in Christ Jesus, [born anew] that we may do those good works which God predestined (planned beforehand) for us [taking paths which He prepared ahead of time], that we should walk in them [living the good life which He prearranged and made ready for us to live].*

You are the "handiwork" of God. He has already planned a good life for you and wants you to walk in it. He wants you to walk out your story with expectancy and enthusiasm. There will be laughter and tears, good times and hard times, but they will work together to weave an amazing story that you can tell. Maybe someday someone will be writing a book and they will find your story on the Internet, copy it, and share it in their book to encourage their readers.

I read that Helen Keller once said, "Life is a succession of lessons which must be lived out to be understood." I think there is real power in that statement. As you walk with God, He will teach you new lessons with each new experience you face. But in order to learn those lessons, it is important that you are living your own story. God is going to continue to teach you, guide you, and bless you, as you live your own life for Him.

Live Your Best Story

All of us have made mistakes in our past—not one of us is perfect. But that doesn't mean we have to repeat those mistakes in the future. The longer you walk with God, the more you learn about His power to help you live a victorious, joy-filled life. You don't have to suffer from the same defeats of yesterday; by the grace of God, you can live differently today. Your story can get better and better—you can learn to live in God's best.

> *You don't have to suffer from the same defeats of yesterday; by the grace of God, you can live differently today.*

I love what the Bible says about living our best life for God...

Whatever may be your task, work at it heartily (from the soul), as [something done] for the Lord and not for men, Knowing [with all certainty] that it is from the Lord [and not from men] that you will receive the inheritance which is your [real] reward. [The One Whom] you are actually serving [is] the Lord Christ (the Messiah). (Colossians 3:23–24)

Concentrate on doing your best for God, work you won't be ashamed of, laying out the truth plain and simple. (2 Timothy 2:15 The Message)

And whatever you do [no matter what it is] in word or deed, do everything in the name of the Lord Jesus and in [dependence upon] His Person, giving praise to God the Father through Him. (Colossians 3:17)

These verses encourage us to do our best for God. When our time on Earth is up and we go to heaven, we should leave behind the story of a life lived for God. It comforts me to know that God doesn't expect perfection; He just asks for my best, whatever that may be.

I'm far from perfect, but I can tell you that I'm a lot better off than I was 20 years ago...10 years ago...and even five years ago. God has taught me so much and done so much in my life. I don't want to waste that. My best life is the life that God prepared me for and the one I'm enjoying today. And you know what? I believe five years from now...10 years from now...and even 20 years from now, I will have learned even more. I'll be living in new levels of victory!

The same is true for you. You may not be where you want to be, but thank God you're not where you used to be. If you let Him, God will continue to develop His character in your life each and every day so you can live your best story for Him and enjoy the life Jesus came to give you. It's all about receiving the best God has to offer and living your life for Him in return.

Sadly, there are a lot of Christians who are giving their best to a career or a worldly endeavor. They give their best time, energy, and focus to a job while their relationship with God gets the leftovers. I believe that's an example of misplaced priorities. God deserves

> *Your job, your family, your attitudes, and your actions all prosper when God is at the center of your life.*

our best every day. I've discovered when you spend the beginning of your day with Him, and when you commit to do your best for Him in everything you do, He blesses everything you put your hand to. Your job, your family, your attitudes, and your actions all prosper when God is at the center of your life.

Live Your New Story

What if instead of writing chapter 17, I decided to just retype chapter 1 and call it chapter 17? I'm sure I'd get a lot of letters from disappointed readers. "Joyce, why in the world didn't you write a new chapter? Why did you just retype an old chapter? We've already read that chapter. We want something new!" And they would be completely correct. It would be a mistake for me to focus on a past chapter. Chapter 1 is over. This is a new chapter. And with each new chapter is an opportunity for both of us—an opportunity to discover something fresh and new.

The same truth that applies to writing a book is true for living your life. The day that lies before you is an unwritten chapter. What words are you going to write on those pages? Are you going to tell us about new hope, new prayers, new victories, and new adventures in God...or are you going to rewrite a page from a previous chapter? The things that happened in your past (whether good or bad) are significant chapters that have led up to this point, but you aren't meant to live in yesterday's pages. It's time to live your new story.

Have you ever met someone (or been someone) who tells the same stories over and over again of what God *used* to do? "The 'Jesus Movement' was wonderful because God did this..." or "It was so wonderful when I was first saved because God did that..." or "The revival services we used to have were so wonderful because God did this…" I have the privilege of taking care of my aunt who is 86 and my mom who is 89, and believe me when I say that I hear a lot of the same stories over and over. They both stay in bed most of the day and they don't have many new stories to tell, so they tell the old ones. It is cute, but it is also sad because it means life is almost over for them.

But your story is far from over, it is still being written, and God wants you to know that He isn't finished yet…He is doing a new thing.

Isaiah 43:19 says:

> *Behold, I am doing a new thing! Now it springs forth; do you not perceive and know it and will you not give heed to it? I will even make a way in the wilderness and rivers in the desert.*

I want to encourage you to ask God to reveal the new thing He is doing in your life. Ask Him to give you new stories—new faith, new answered prayers, new dependence on Him, and new opportunities to make a difference in the world around you. Today is the perfect day to begin again with God. You don't have to live on what used to be. You can write a new chapter for your family, for your church, for your career, for your community, and for your life with the Lord. *Behold, He is doing a new thing!*

> *Today is the perfect day to begin again with God.*

Live God's Bigger Story

I began this book by writing that *it's never too late* is one of the core messages of the Bible, and as I type these final words, I'm reminded of that once again. We've talked a lot about fresh starts and new beginnings, about overcoming obstacles and discovering destiny, but none of that happens apart from the greater story being told. The reason why it's not too late for you is because the story of Jesus' dying on the cross to pay for our sins and His resurrection from the dead is the greatest story ever told, and it is His story that makes our stories possible.

In the pages of the Bible, God's story and our story collide. Humanity was broken and without hope, scarred by the self-inflicted wounds of sin, but God loved us even in our lowest state. He refused to give up on us even when we had given up on ourselves. He sprang into action, laying out His great rescue plan: Jesus. When our story collides with His, it is resolved!

The cross of Calvary forever echoes through the corridors of time: No matter who you are, no matter what you've done, it's never too late to begin again. The prophet Isaiah tells us, "Though your sins are like scarlet, they shall be as white as snow" (Isaiah 1:18), and the apostle Paul exhorts us, "If anyone is in Christ, he is a new creation" (2 Corinthians 5:17 NKJV). These verses show us that salvation is a fresh sunrise, a clean canvas, a new beginning.

> *The cross of Calvary forever echoes through the corridors of time: No matter who you are, no matter what you've done, it's never too late to begin again.*

Let me remind you again that your story is only possible because of God's story. His love for you, His pursuit of you, and His grace for you changed the narrative. You're no longer subject to the bondage of sin. You don't have to live in fear or worry one day longer. You are redeemed through grace by faith in Jesus. That means your life is forever changed. Peace, rest, and joy are yours for the taking. Your life can be different from what it used to be. Your life can be the joy-filled, overcoming, abundant life Jesus came to give you. If you haven't lived in the truth of that promise, you can start today.

IT'S NEVER TOO LATE!!

Summary:

- There is tremendous power in your story.
- Reject the temptation to compare your life to someone else's. God is doing something powerful in your story.
- God gave His best for you; choose to give your very best to Him.
- Today is a new day in your life. Ask God for new stories of victory in Him.
- Your story is only possible because of Jesus. His love for you is the greatest story ever told.

IT'S NEVER TOO LATE TO . . .

- ✓ Give Back
- ✓ Receive Grace
- ✓ Tell Someone You're Proud Of Them
- ✓ Have Childlike Faith
- ✓ Take Time For Yourself
- ✓ Do Great Things
- ✓ Be The Parent God Has Called You To Be
- ✓ Go Back To School
- ✓ Say "I Love You"
- ✓ Stand Up For What You Believe
- ✓ Show Kindness To Another
- ✓ Earn Trust
- ✓ Start That Career
- ✓ Obey The Lord
- ✓ Set Boundaries
- ✓ Join A Gym
- ✓ Pursue Your Dream

AFTERWORD

Congratulations! You made it to the end of *You Can Begin Again*. (If you're like me, you feel a small sense of accomplishment when you finish a book.) I hope you enjoyed reading this book, because I certainly enjoyed writing it. Every page was carefully thought out, and every word was prayerfully written. And from page one until now, my desire has been that you would do more than just hear from me—my desire has been that you would hear from the Lord.

We've covered a lot of material during our time together. Stories were told, applications were made, challenges were given, and scriptures were studied. (By my count, there are nearly 200 different Bible verses or Bible stories shared in this book.) Because the Word of God never returns void (Isaiah 55:11), I trust that God has spoken some things to your heart in one or more of the pages you've read. I believe the Holy Spirit has done something powerful in your life, and if it's possible, I'm just as excited about that as you are!

But, before you put this book on the shelf, I want to say one last thing...

God put this book in your hands because He loves you greatly, and since you are part of His story, it is important for you to remember when one of those hard days comes along and you feel like you may not make it, it is only one page in the story of your life; it is not the whole story, so turn the page and keep writing.

PRAYER OF SALVATION

The most important relationship of your life is a personal relationship with Jesus Christ. If you would like to receive Him as your
Lord and Savior and enter into the greatest relationship you have
ever known, please pray the prayer below:

Father,

You loved the world so much You gave Your only
begotten Son to die for our sins so that whoever believes
in Him will not perish but have eternal life.

Your Word says we are saved by grace through faith
as a gift from You. There is nothing we can do to earn
salvation.

I believe and confess with my mouth that Jesus Christ
is Your Son, the Savior of the world. I believe He died on
the cross for me and bore all of my sins, paying the price
for them.

I believe in my heart that You raised Jesus from the dead
and that He is alive today.

I am a sinner; I am sorry for my sins; and I ask You to
forgive me. By faith, I receive Jesus Christ now as my
Lord and Savior. I believe that I am saved and will spend
eternity with You! Thank You, Father. I am so grateful!
In Jesus' name, Amen.

ABOUT THE AUTHOR

JOYCE MEYER is one of the world's leading practical Bible teachers. Her TV and radio broadcast, *Enjoying Everyday Life*, airs on hundreds of television networks and radio stations worldwide.

Joyce has written more than 100 inspirational books. Her bestsellers include *God Is Not Mad at You*; *Making Good Habits, Breaking Bad Habits*; *Do Yourself a Favor...Forgive*; *Living Beyond Your Feelings*; *Power Thoughts*; *Battlefield of the Mind*; *Look Great, Feel Great*; *The Confident Woman*; *I Dare You*; and *Never Give Up!*

Joyce travels extensively, holding conferences throughout the year, and speaking to thousands around the world.

JOYCE MEYER MINISTRIES U.S. & FOREIGN OFFICE ADDRESSES

Joyce Meyer Ministries
P.O. Box 655
Fenton, MO 63026
USA
(636) 349-0303

Joyce Meyer Ministries—Canada
P.O. Box 7700
Vancouver, BC V6B 4E2
Canada
(800) 868-1002

Joyce Meyer Ministries—Australia
Locked Bag 77
Mansfield Delivery Centre
Queensland 4122
Australia
(07) 3349 1200

Joyce Meyer Ministries—England
P.O. Box 1549
Windsor SL4 1GT
United Kingdom
01753 831102

Joyce Meyer Ministries—South Africa
P.O. Box 5
Cape Town 8000
South Africa
(27) 21-701-1056

OTHER BOOKS BY JOYCE

*Battlefield of the Mind** (over three million copies sold)
*God Is Not Mad at You**
*Making Good Habits, Breaking Bad Habits**
*Do Yourself a Favor...Forgive**
*Power Thoughts**
*Living Beyond Your Feelings**
*Eat the Cookie...Buy the Shoes**
Never Give Up!
I Dare You
The Penny
The Power of Simple Prayer
*The Confident Woman**
Look Great, Feel Great
*Approval Addiction**
*The Love Revolution**
Any Minute
Start Your New Life Today
21 Ways to Finding Peace and Happiness
A New Way of Living
Woman to Woman
100 Ways to Simplify Your Life
The Secret to True Happiness
Reduce Me to Love
The Secret Power of Speaking God's Word

Devotionals

Love Out Loud Devotional
The Confident Woman Devotional
Hearing from God Each Morning

New Day, New You Devotional
Battlefield of the Mind Devotional
*Ending Your Day Right**
*Starting Your Day Right**

*Also available in Spanish